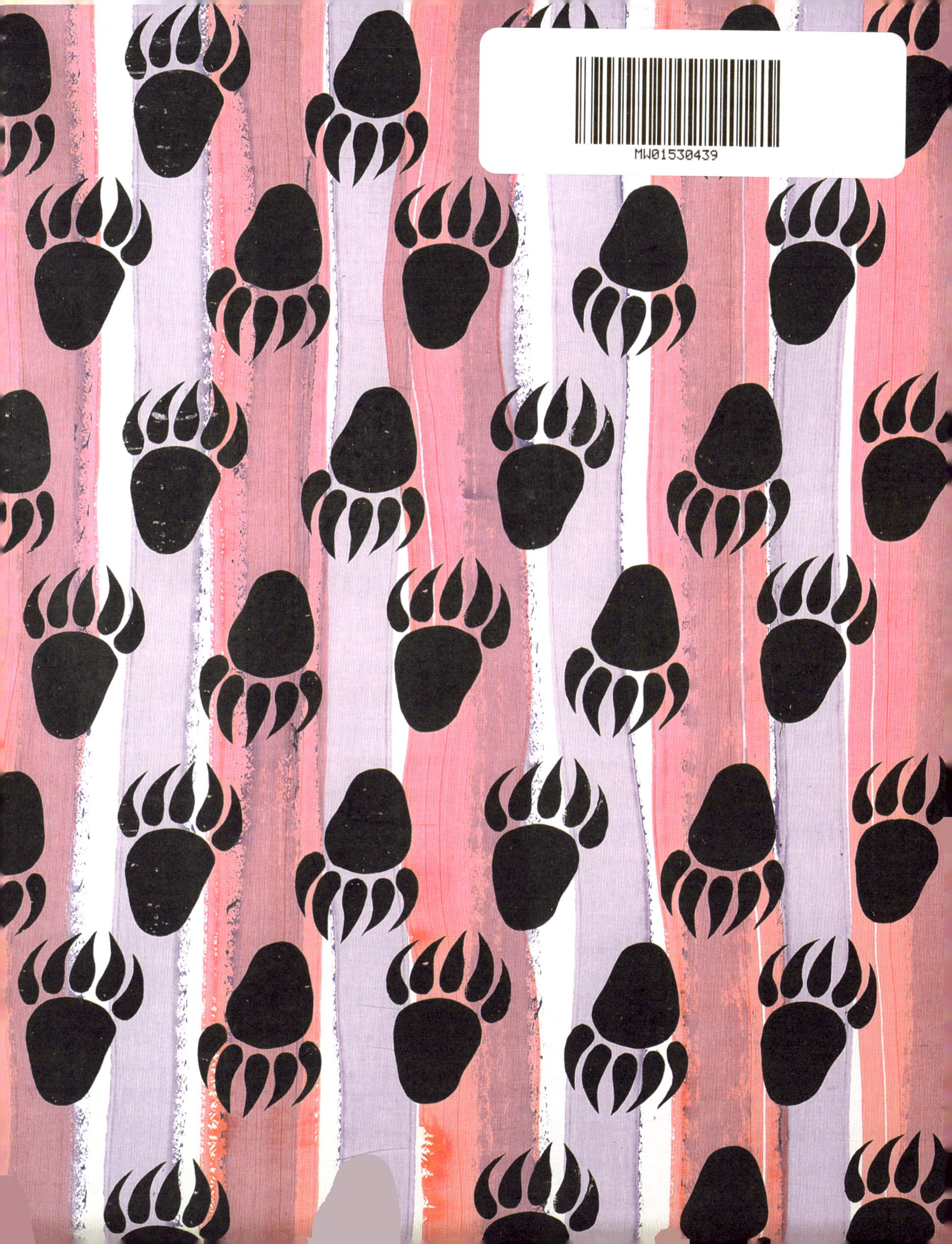

A JOURNAL BY

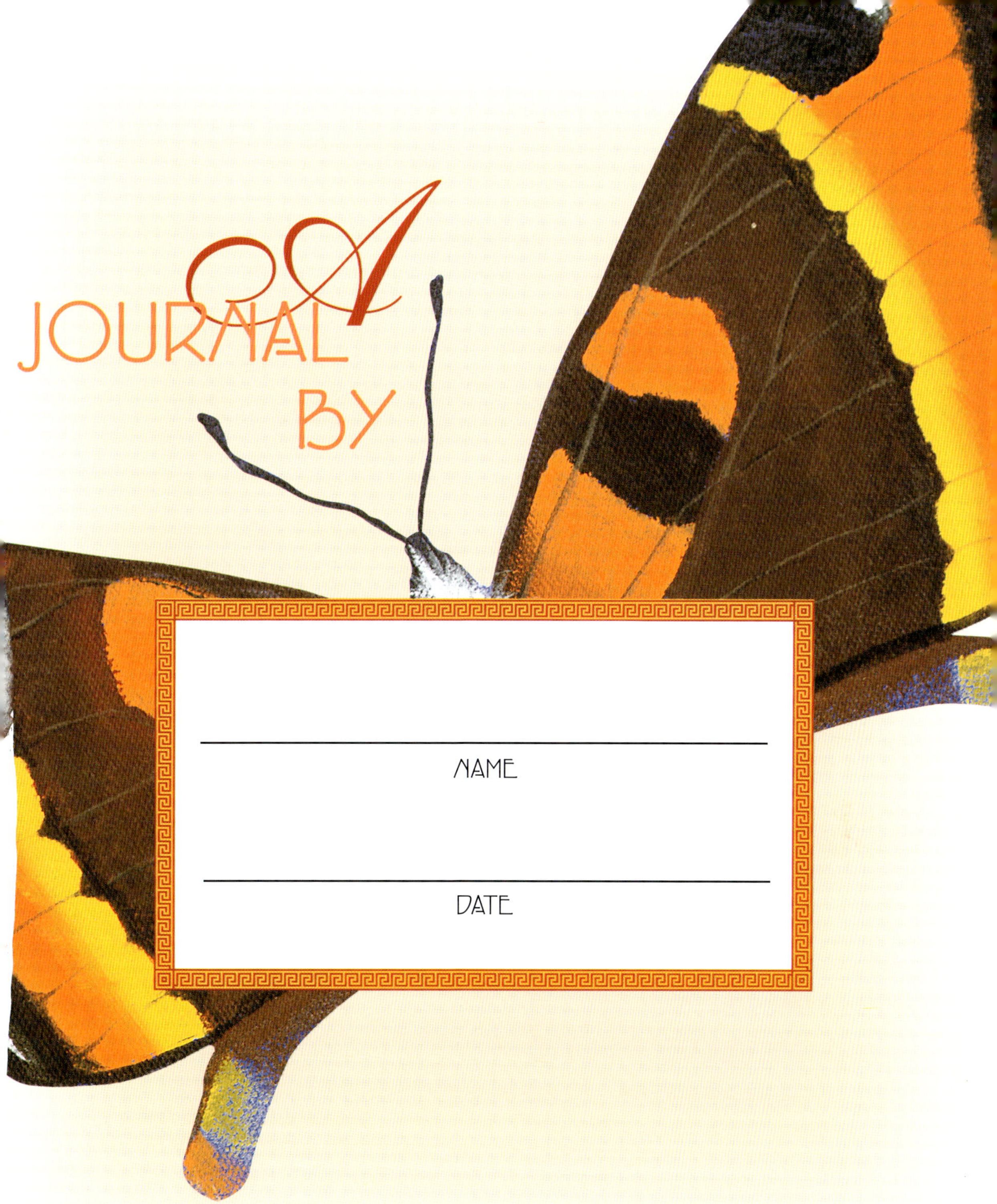

NAME

DATE

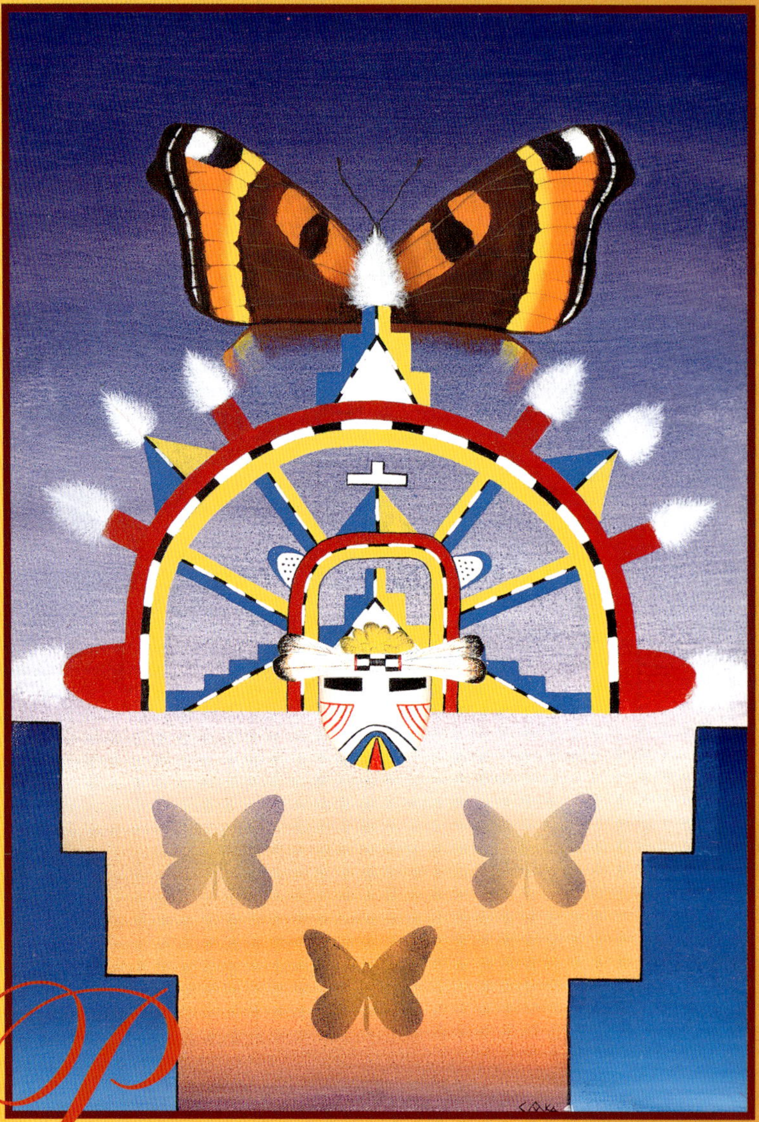

Butterfly Dancer
by Terrence Cooka
(Laguna)
Acrylic on canvas,
26″ x 19″, 1991

Pollen-dusted wings glisten near the stream, and
there is a soft fluttering sound.
In a instant
she is a blue flash,
and then gone.

Dreams & Visions
Pathways to the spirit

Many animal legends and stories speak of fantastic magical events and profound spiritual transformations. They reflect with great beauty and wonder the importance of animals in our lives, and elucidate their many contributions to our world.

Some of these ancient legends teach lessons of compassion, kindness and generosity, with animal-beings bestowing upon humans such gifts as wisdom, insight and patience.

Animals have long been at the center of virtually all tribal philosophies and have been the focus of multitudes of religious functions, providing many guided pathways for those seeking to live in harmony with nature and Mother Earth. Animals are our true relations, with whom we share our homes, our history, our ceremonial and spiritual pursuits, and our challenges and triumphs…and to whom we so often look for direction, and assurance of our continued survival.

*Floating in a large pond
of clear water,
I think of poems I will
write later.*

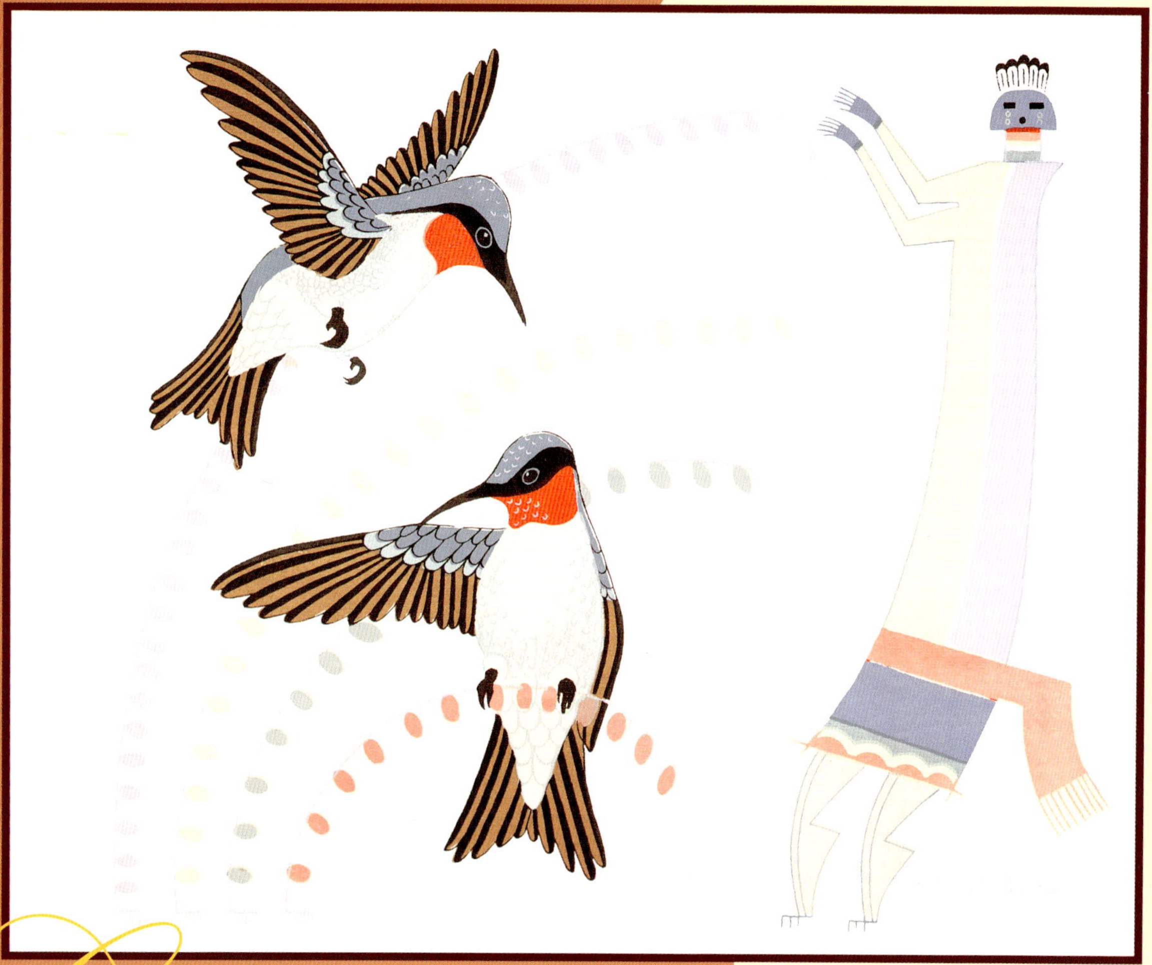

Corn and squash
flower yellow and orange
in the garden.
I have set a bowl of sweet water out
for you,
my tiny sky-gem sisters…
to thank you for these colors.

Hummingbirds
by Gerald Nailor (Navajo)
silkscreen,
10″ x 12″, 1991

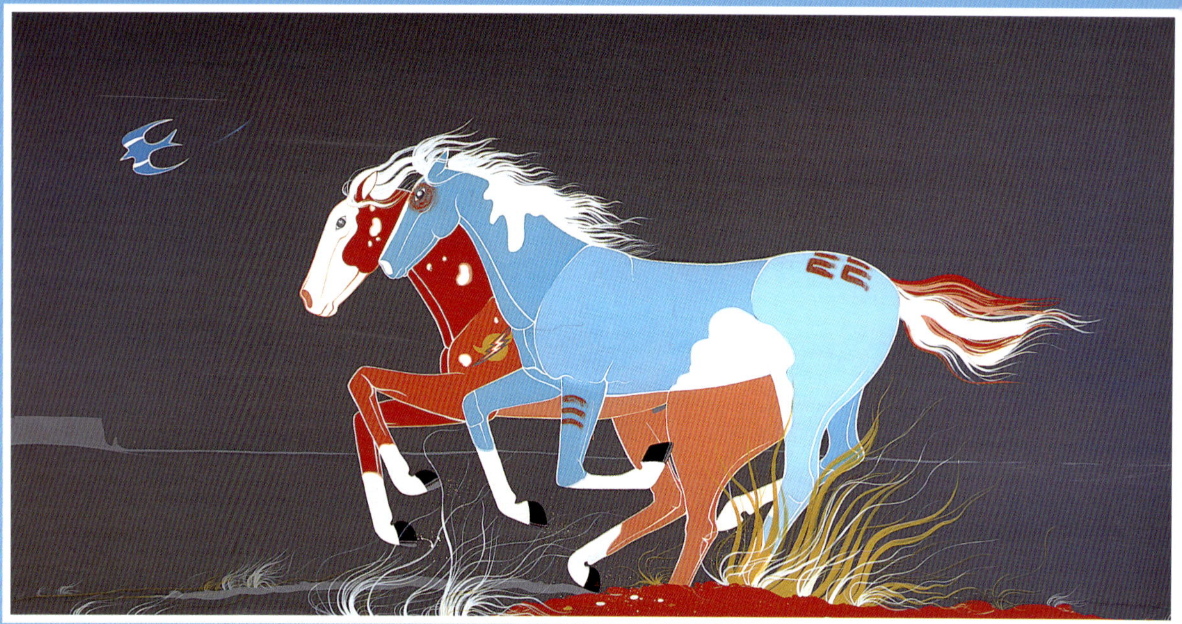

The horses were red and the horses were blue,
carried by ancient winds
into forever's horizon.

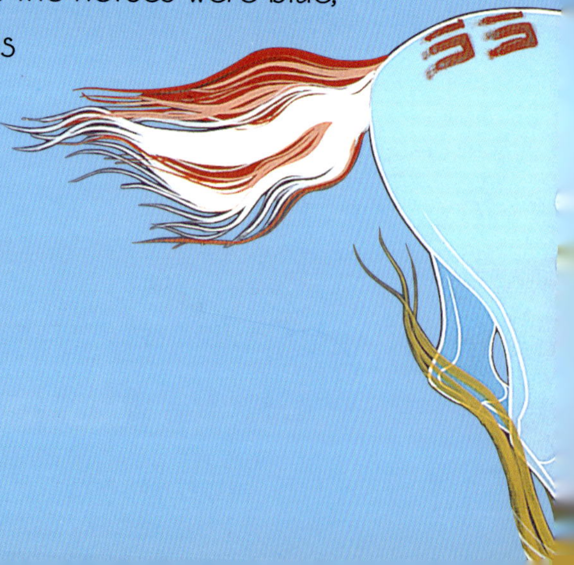

Untitled
by Art Chischilly (Navajo)
oil on board,
49″ x 97″, 1971

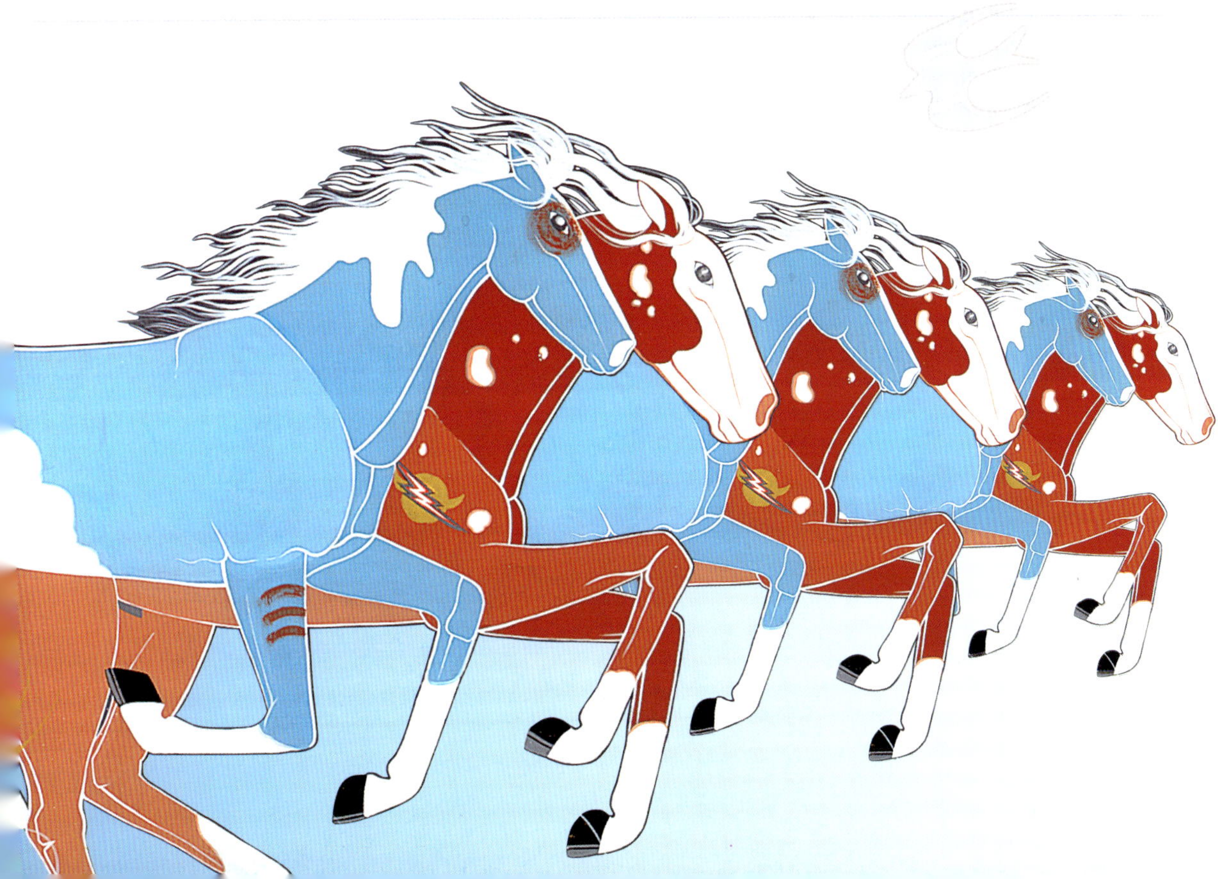

*Candles burn to nothingness
in the empty space of my room.
I awake, the pen still
in my hand,
after dreaming of you again.*

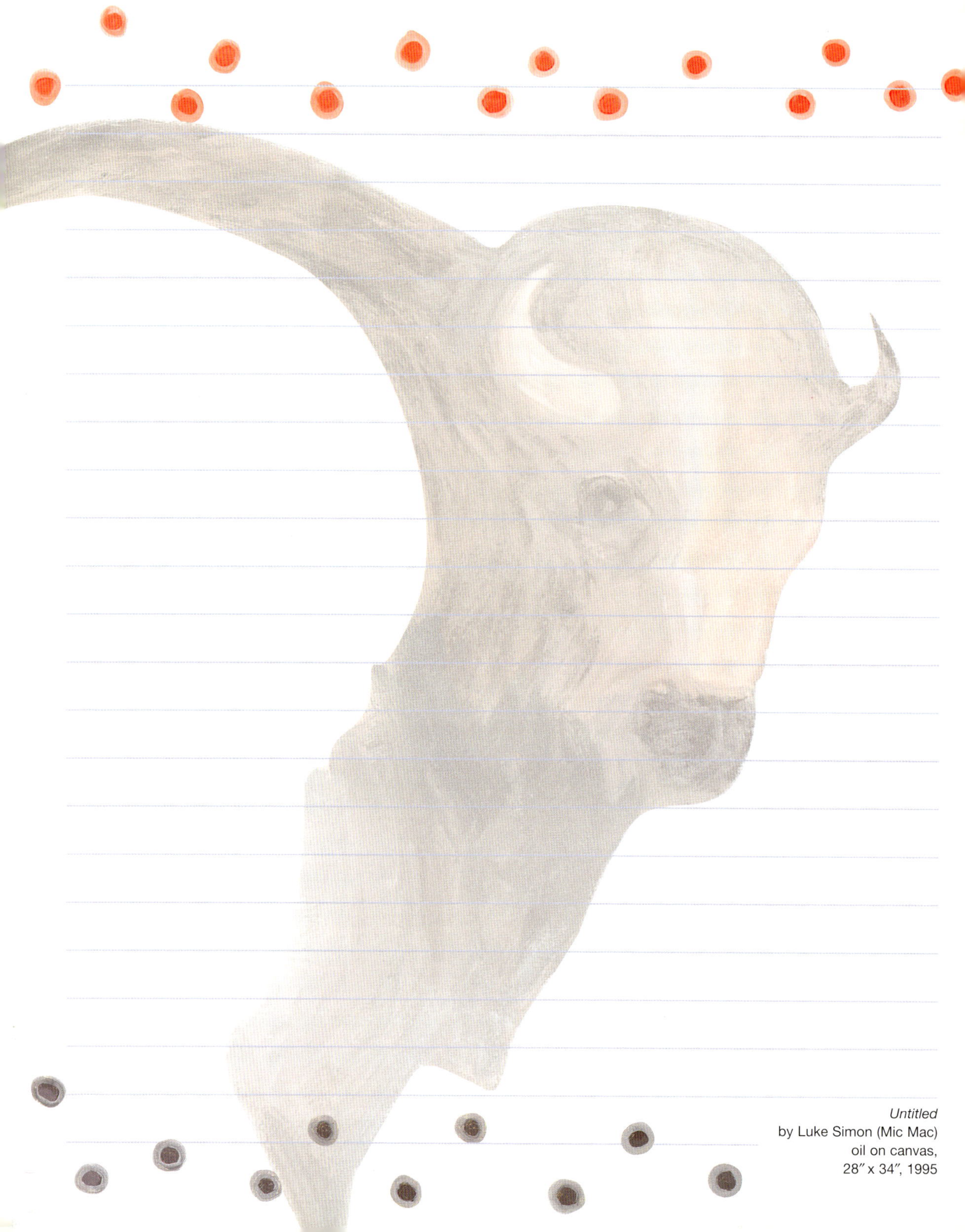

Untitled
by Luke Simon (Mic Mac)
oil on canvas,
28″ x 34″, 1995

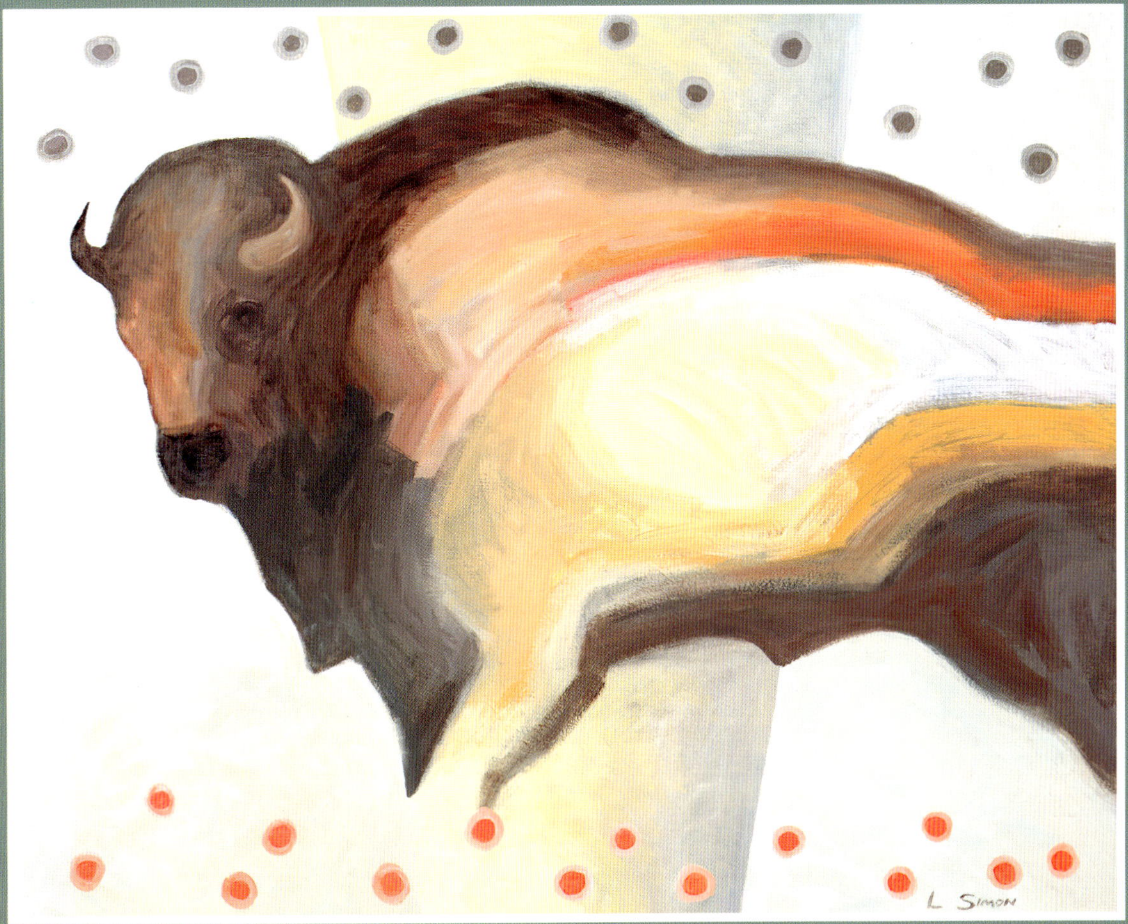
L Simon

Moving east
under new moon's light
there is only the sound
of our breath, and the occasional
whisper of a falling star.

*Lilies from a friend
last a week,
then drop to the tile
below their vase.
I have been writing all night;
seven lilies,
seven poems.*

*I set baskets of resonation at your feet, but
you only laugh at my songs and walk away.*

*When the words do not come easily
you will return to the baskets,
wanting for my words.*

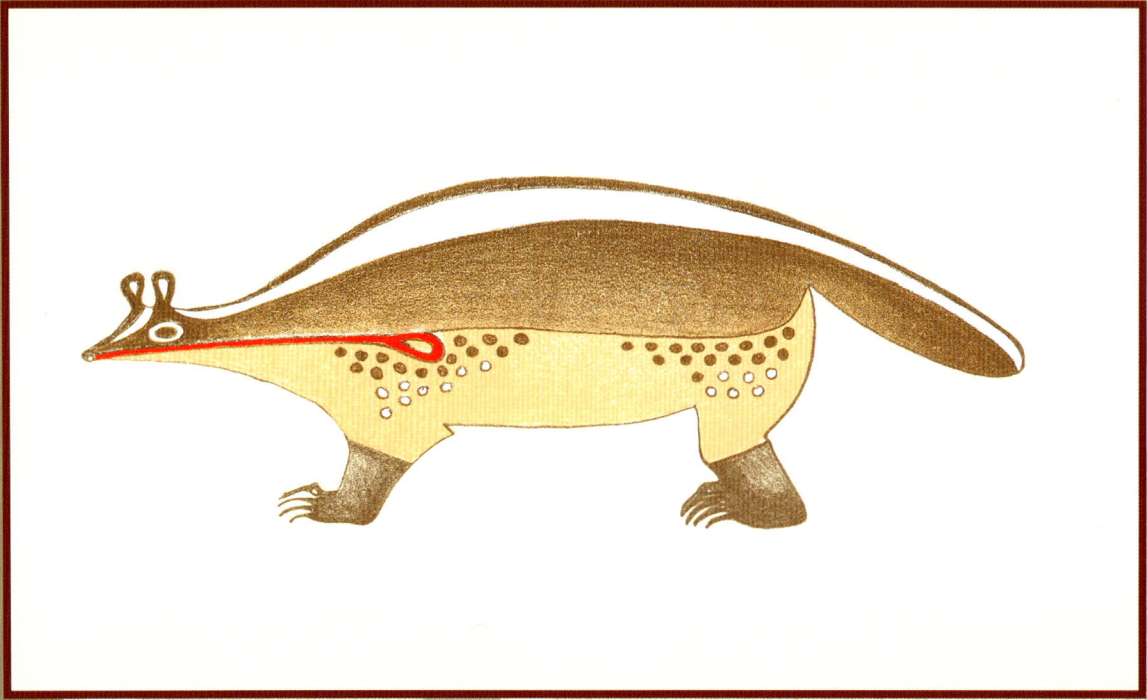

*S*mall circular patterns rest
in the fine sand
near lake's edge.

This is where skunk has walked.

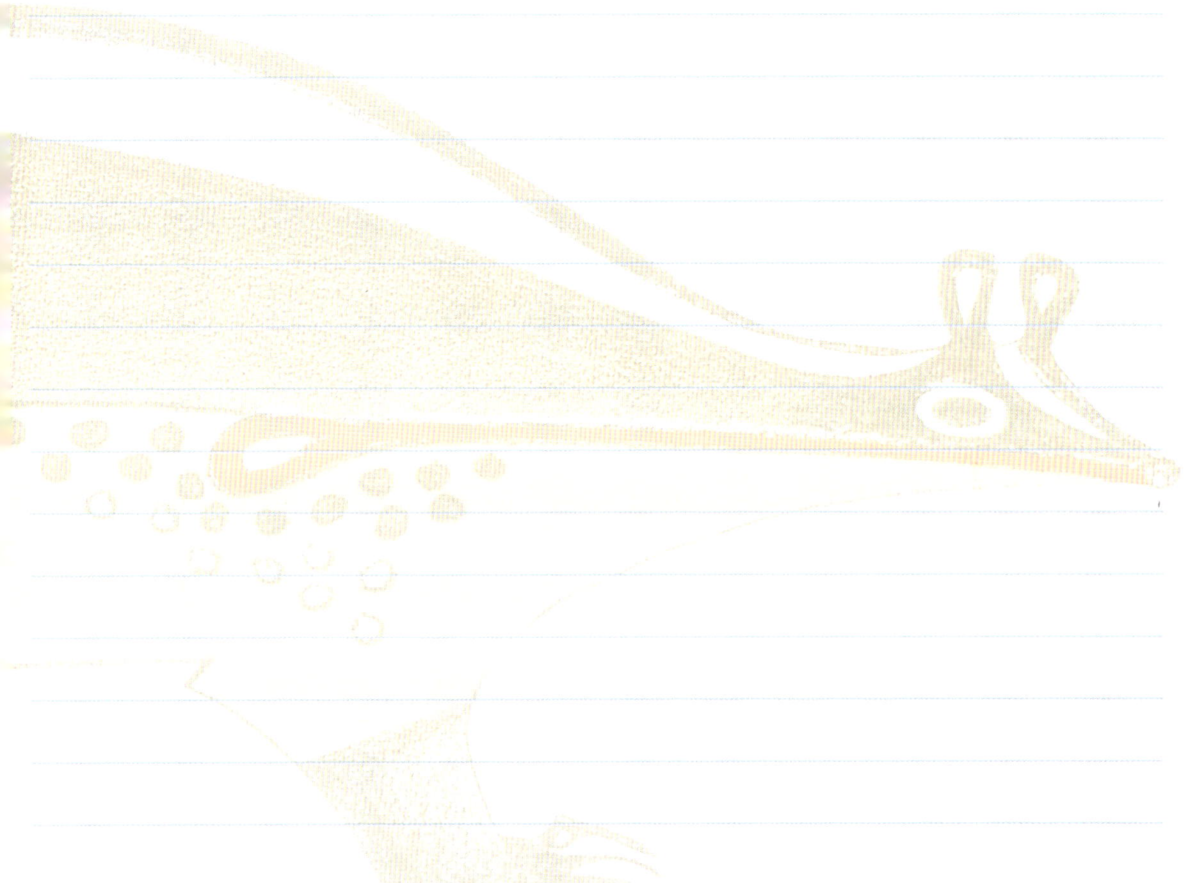

Untitled
by Charles Loloma (Hopi)
lithograph,
9″ x 13 1/2″, 1992

Early morning shadows rise on the wall
while I sit writing prose.
By noon the shadows are gone,
yet I have written only one verse.

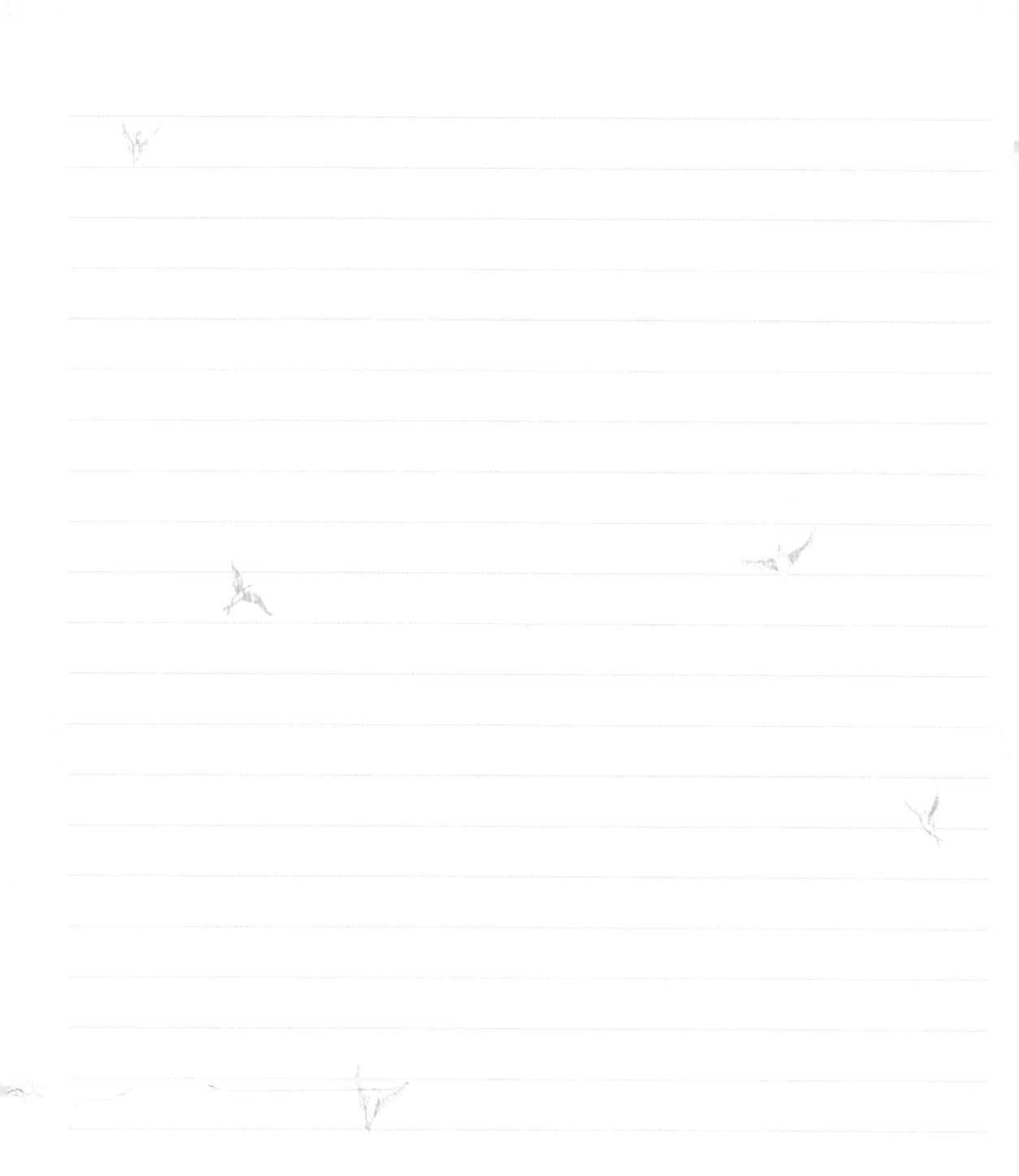

Playing with Watermelons
by Marvin Toddy (Navajo)
Tempera painting,
14¼"x 16", 1991

*S*ummer harvests are sweet and ripe,
    lending invitation for feasting
    and joyous occasion.

M. Tabby

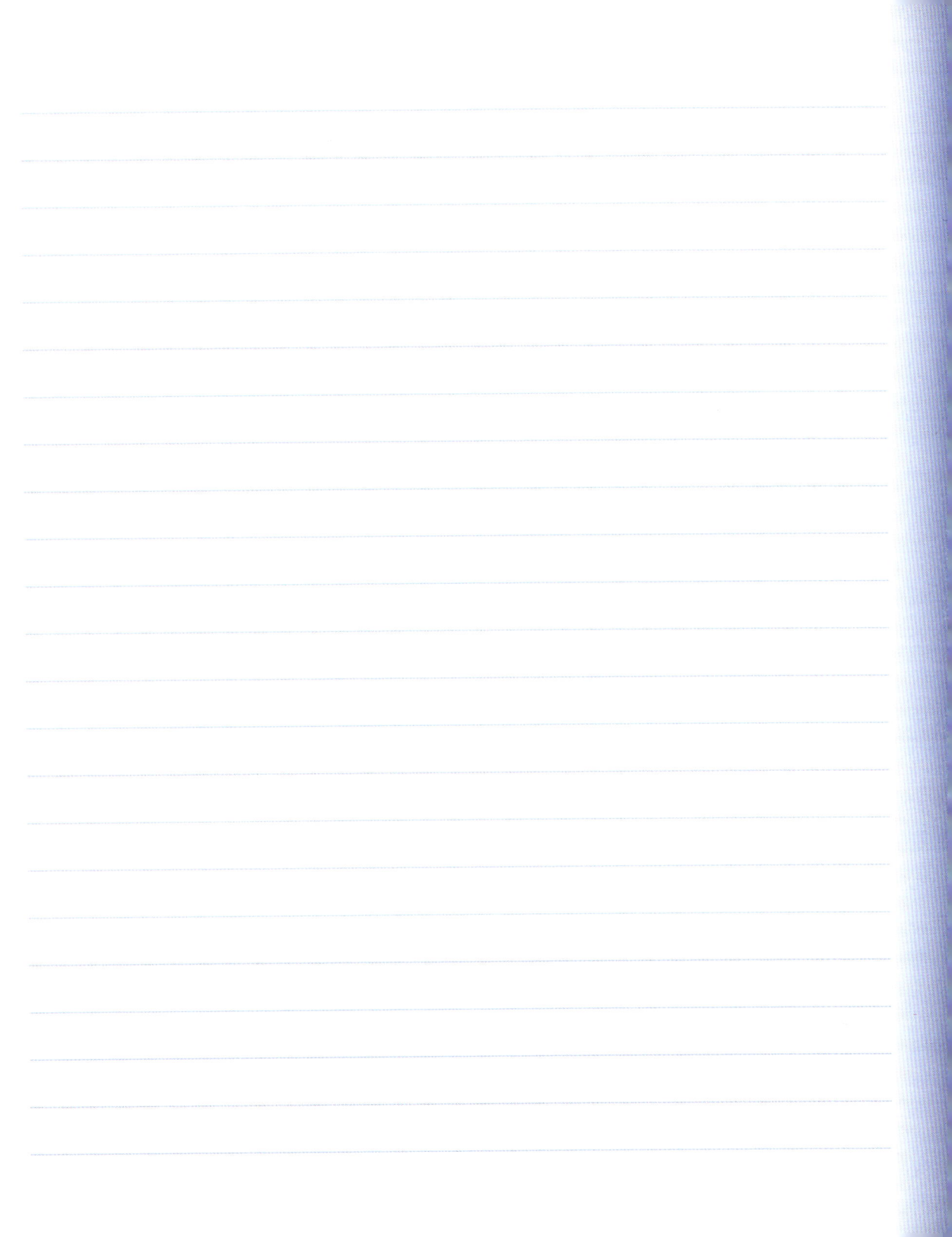

Two dragonflies have landed on my diary
as I sit writing near the pond.
When the last word is written,
only one dragonfly remains.

Sacred prayers rise from eagle's wings,
asking Creator for strength and peace.

The silence between drumbeats
waits for my voice; I watch eagle move.

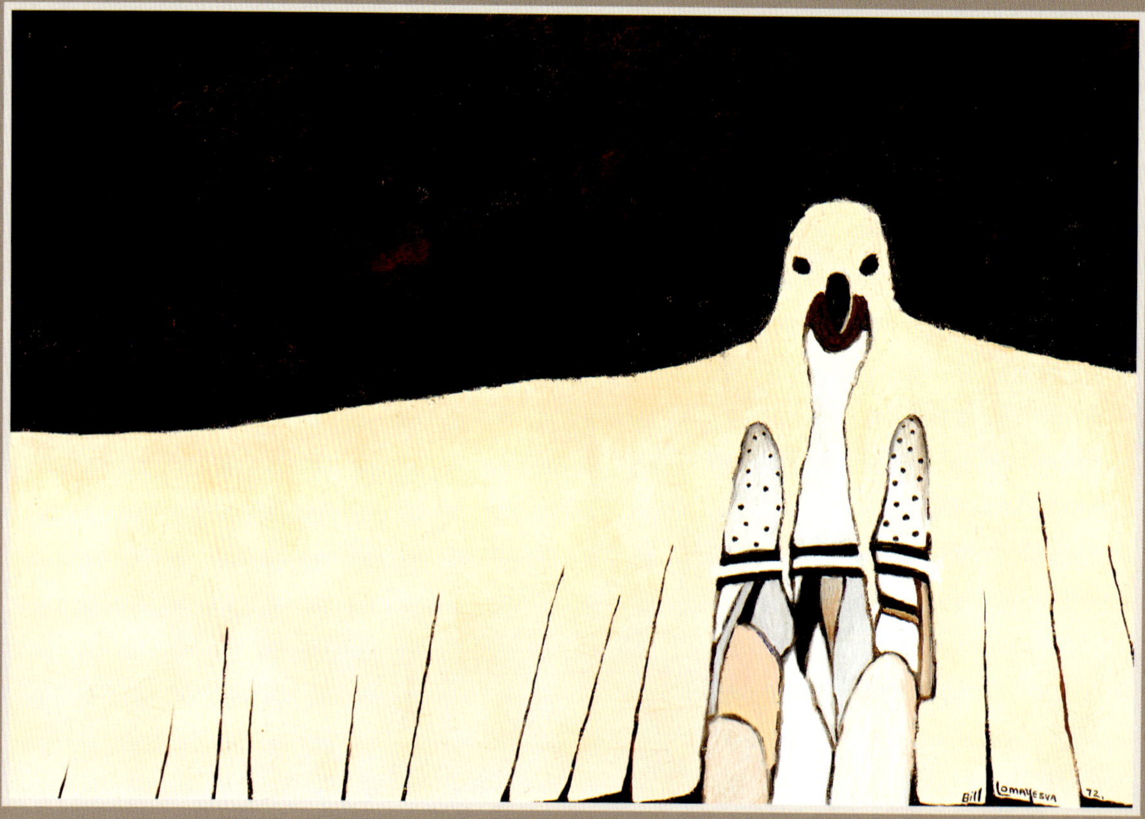
Bill Lomayesva 72.

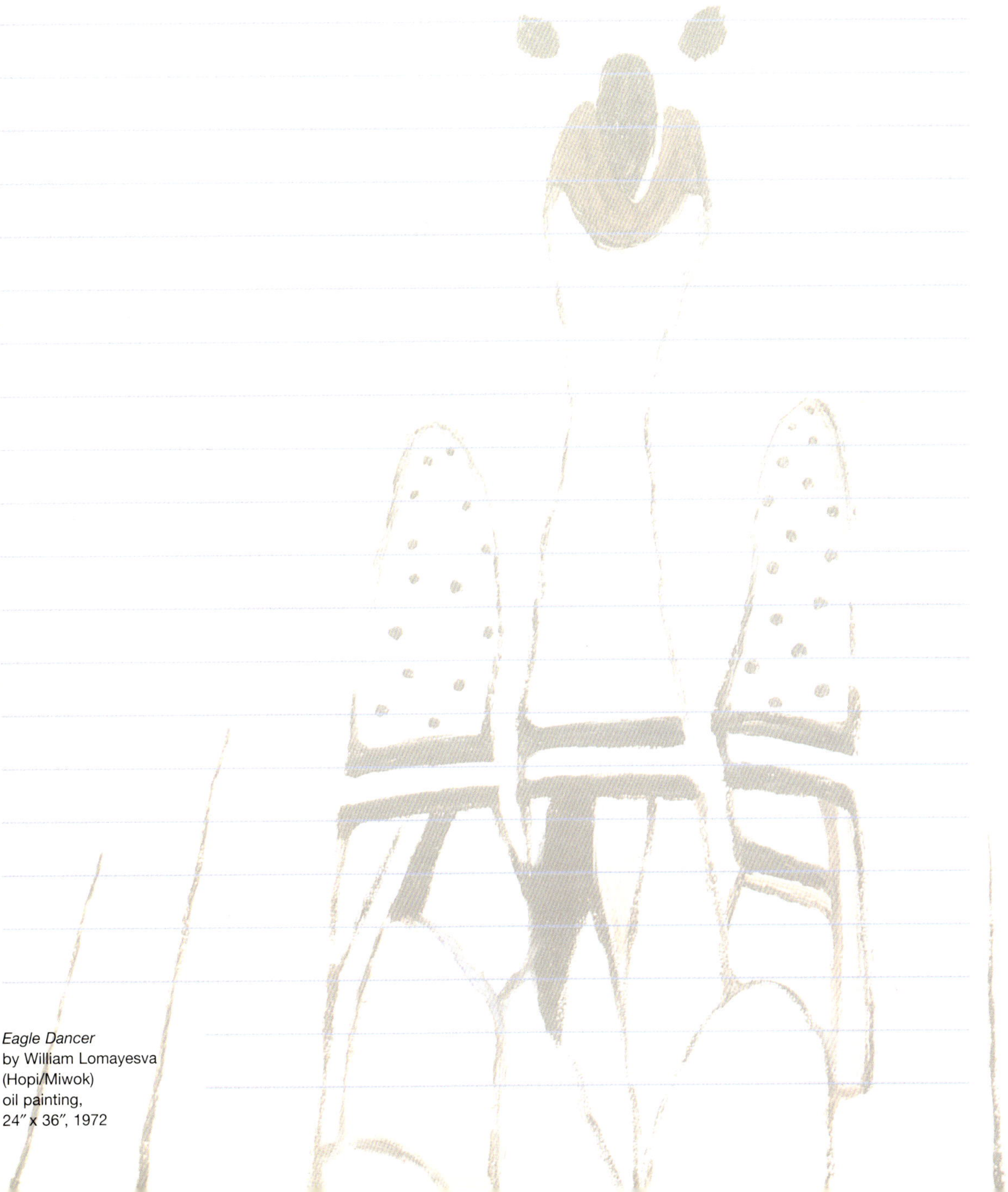

Eagle Dancer
by William Lomayesva
(Hopi/Miwok)
oil painting,
24″ x 36″, 1972

I am surrounded by stillness, and I am completely alone.
Tomorrow I will write again;
three or four poems.

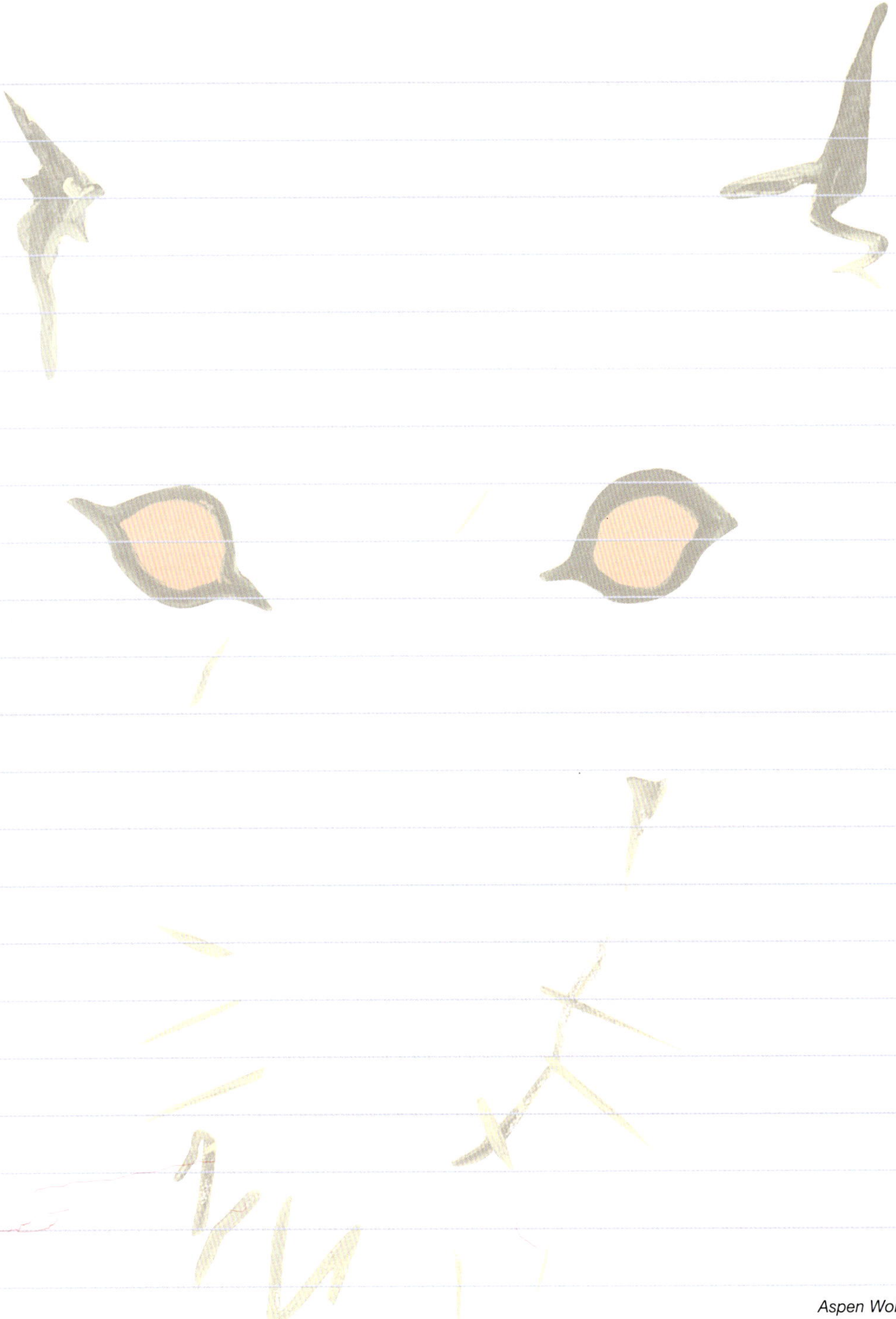

Aspen Wolf Series #1
by Bill Soza
(Cahuilla/Apache)
oil on canvas,
42″ x 32″, 1992

At
aybreak
e is cautious.
/hen night falls
e is swift.
nder moonlight
e is silent,

nis wisdom
eeper of mine.

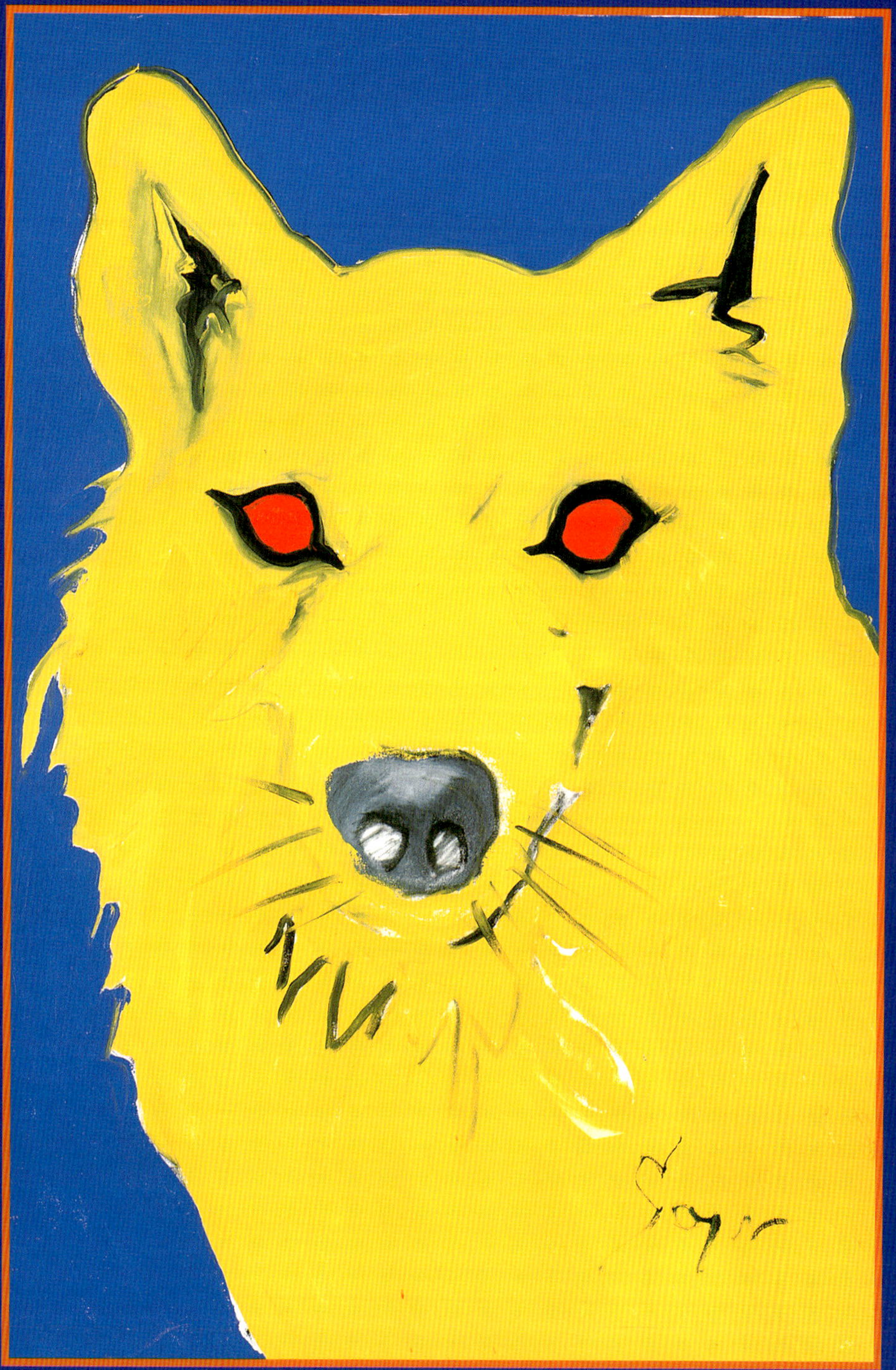

Beads scattered on the table wait to become a necklace. Incense becomes ash, and words wait for the page.

Flighted brother
waits
near a carefully prepared nest.
Soon,
she will return
and the season of new life
will begin.

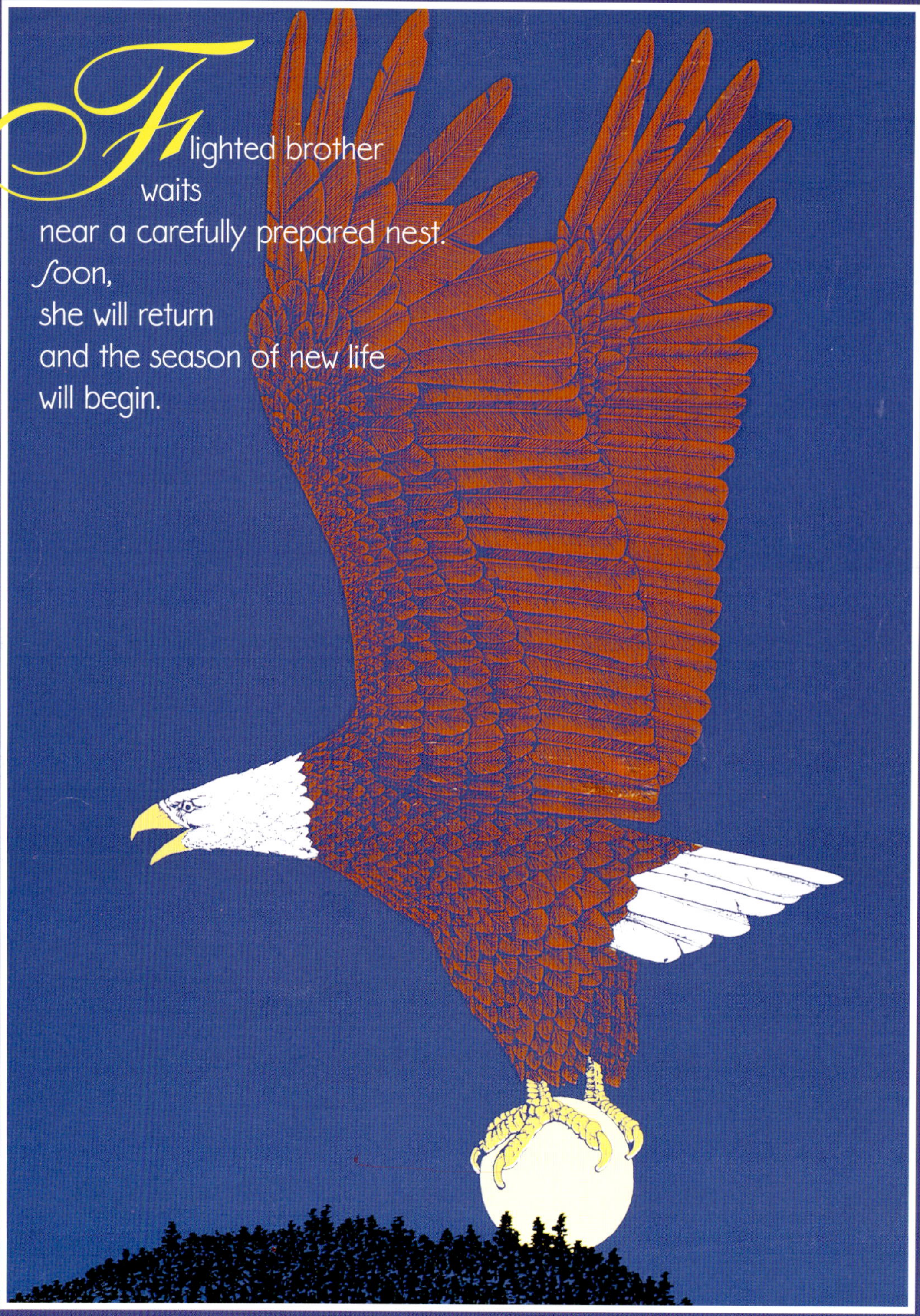

The Eagle Has Landed
by Robert Hill (NTA)
lithograph,
33 1/4″ x 25″, 1998

Even the silence of winter holds the spirit of creativity.

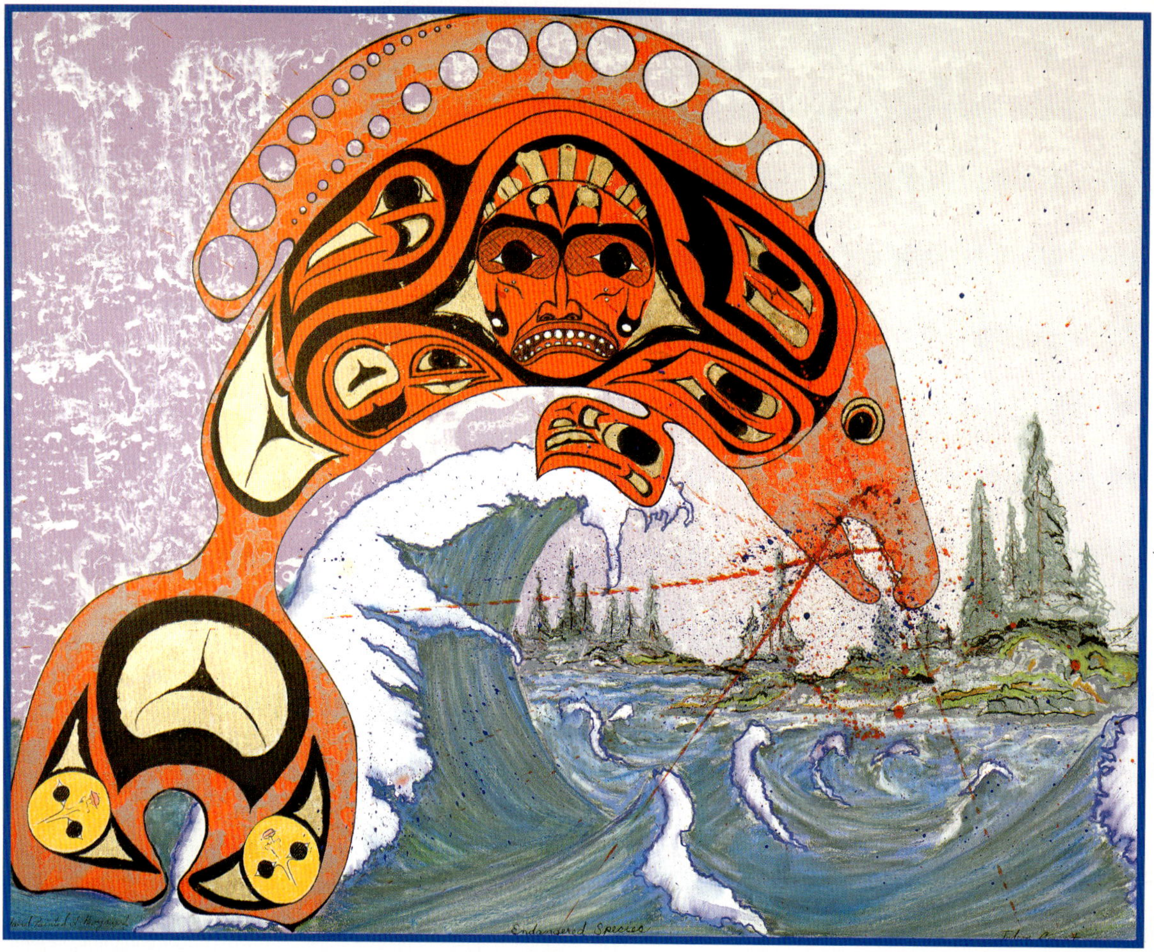
Endangered Species

Salmon streams
overflow with life;
blue-green waves
reflect only
what the soul
wishes to see.

Endangered Specie
by Judson Cransto
(Tlingit/Haida)
lithograph,
28″ x 37″, 1996

Fog rises above the mountain's peak.
I am without you
and I am writing poetry.

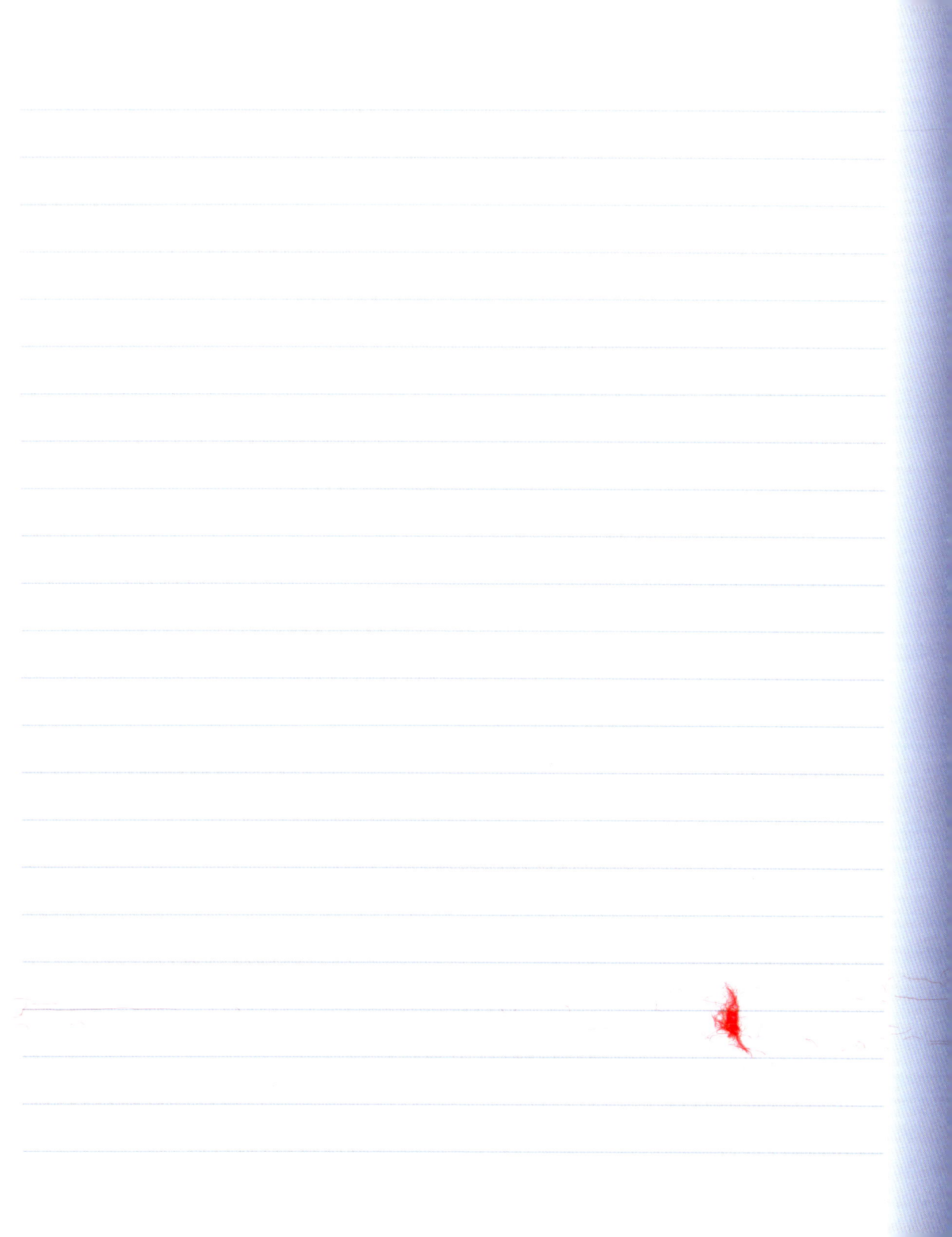

To the north,
mountains and lakes;
toward the east, large bear and
buffalo shadows.

Abstracted landscapes
in the places remaining.

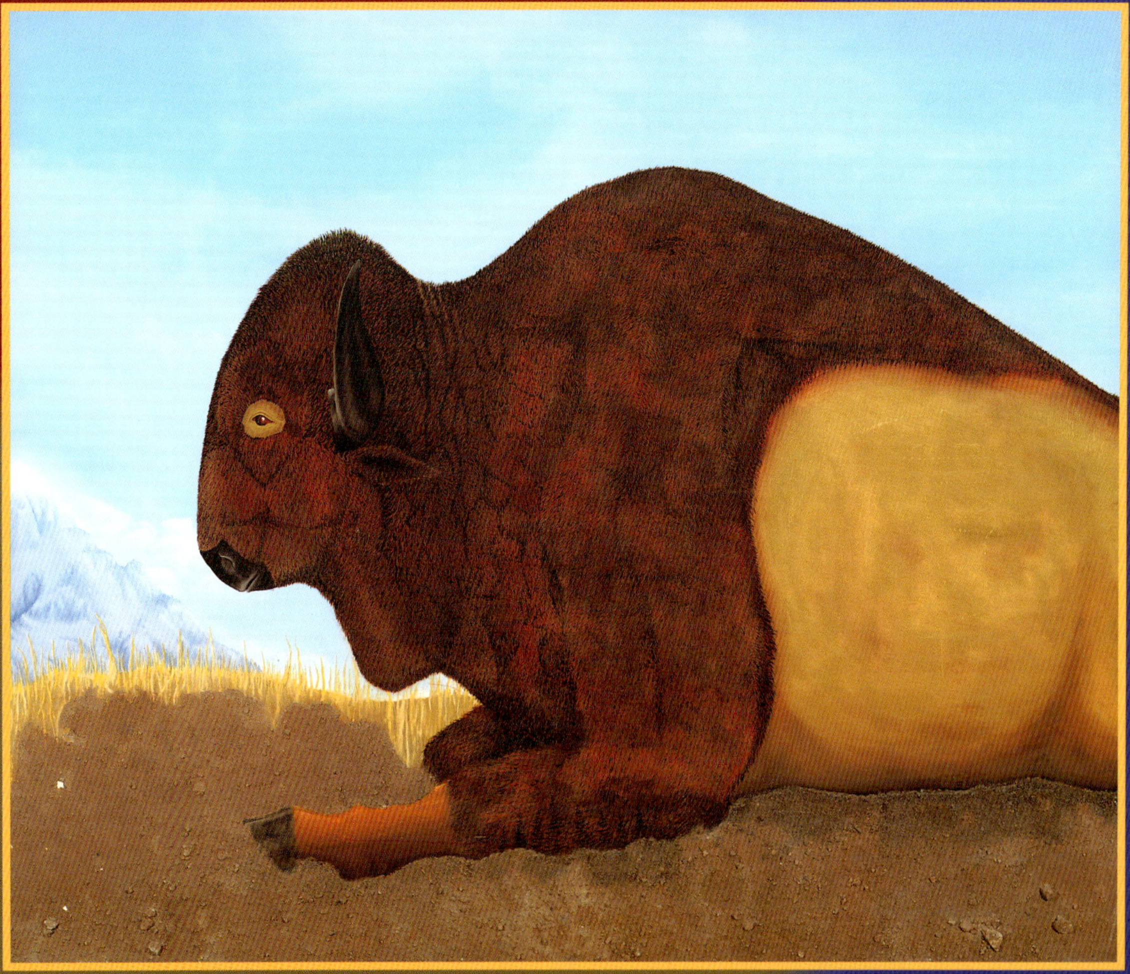

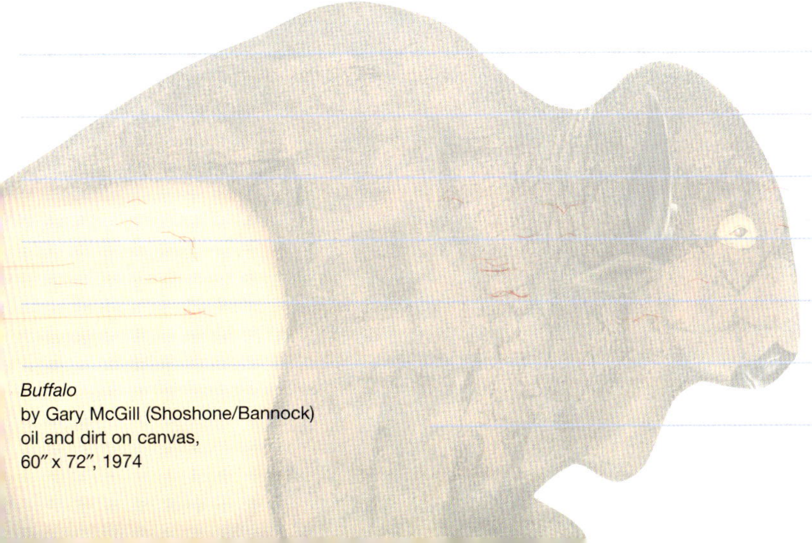

Buffalo
by Gary McGill (Shoshone/Bannock)
oil and dirt on canvas,
60″ x 72″, 1974

Fall has arrived.
Soon there will be snow, and
new stories will be born.

*G*reen flash
against hot silver
granite. Hopping
from ledge to ledge
gecko is quick and light

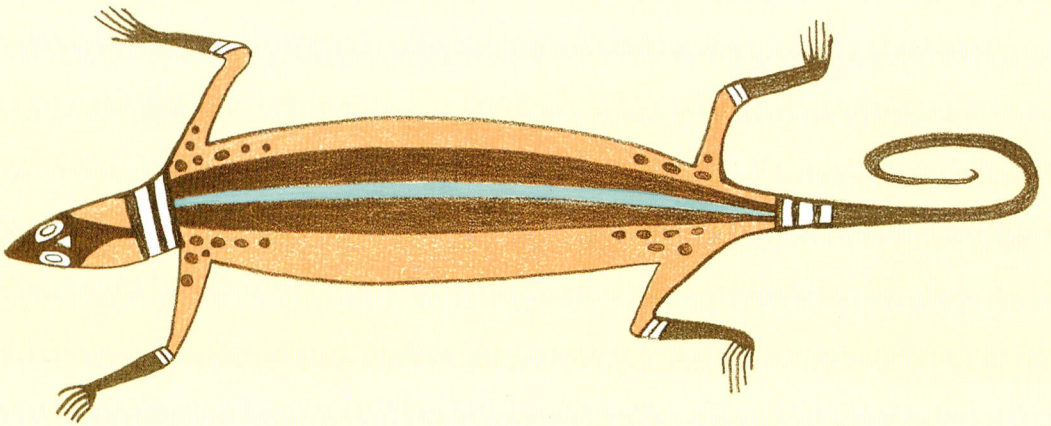

Father Lizard
by Charles Loloma (Hopi)
Lithograph,
9″ x 13½″, 1992

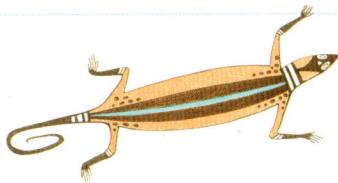

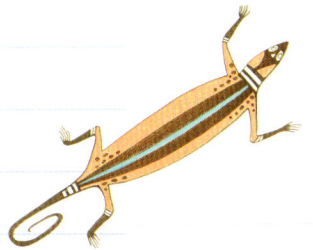

A storm builds in the distance;
it is time for rain.
Water glistens on the sill;
I wait for the ink to warm.

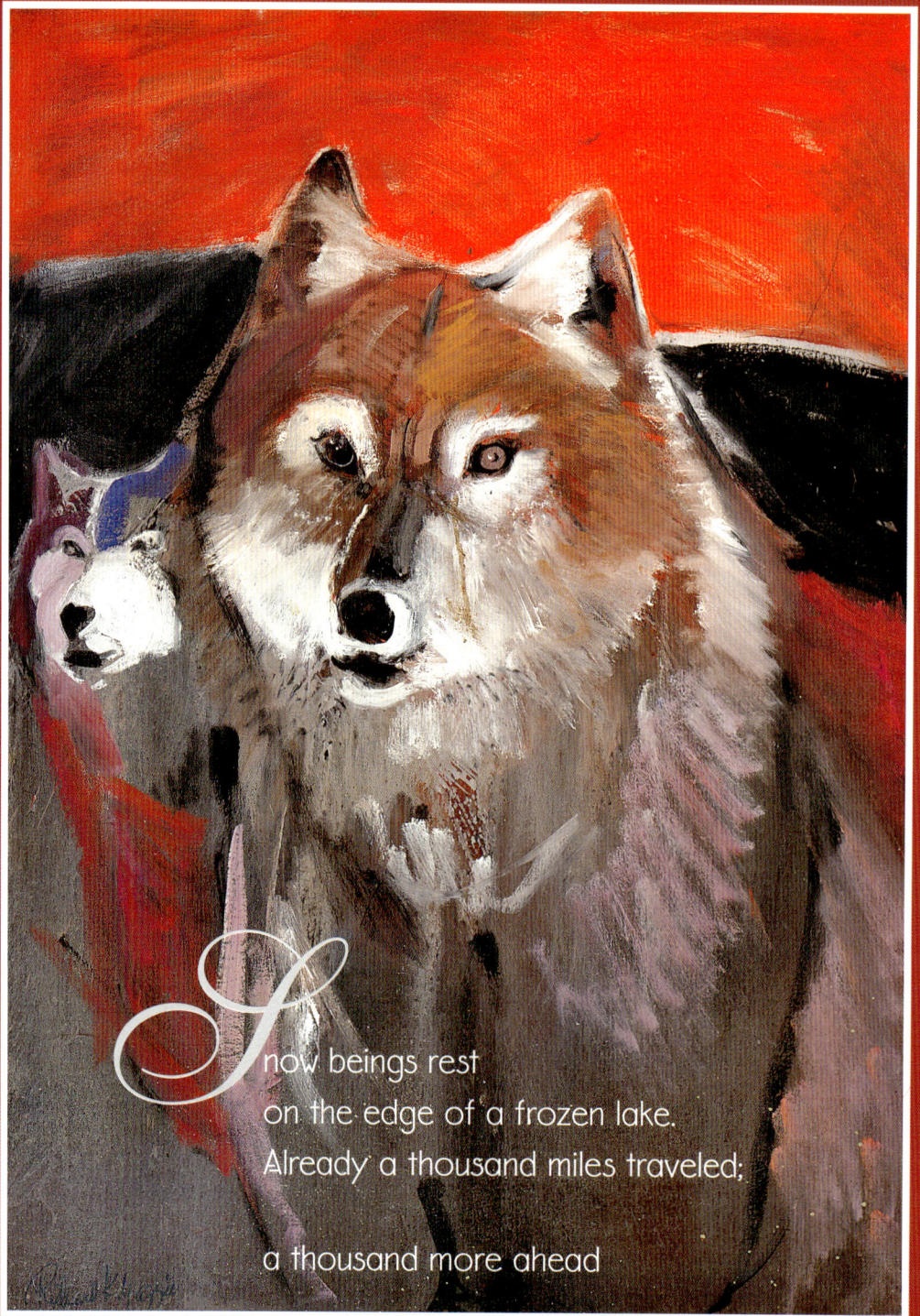

*S*now beings rest
on the edge of a frozen lake.
Already a thousand miles traveled;

a thousand more ahead

Two Huskies
by Richard Yazzie
(Navajo)
oil painting,
37″ x 27″, 1968

A footprint on the walk
tells me she was here.
A note on the door
says she will return;

she is ready to read what I have written.

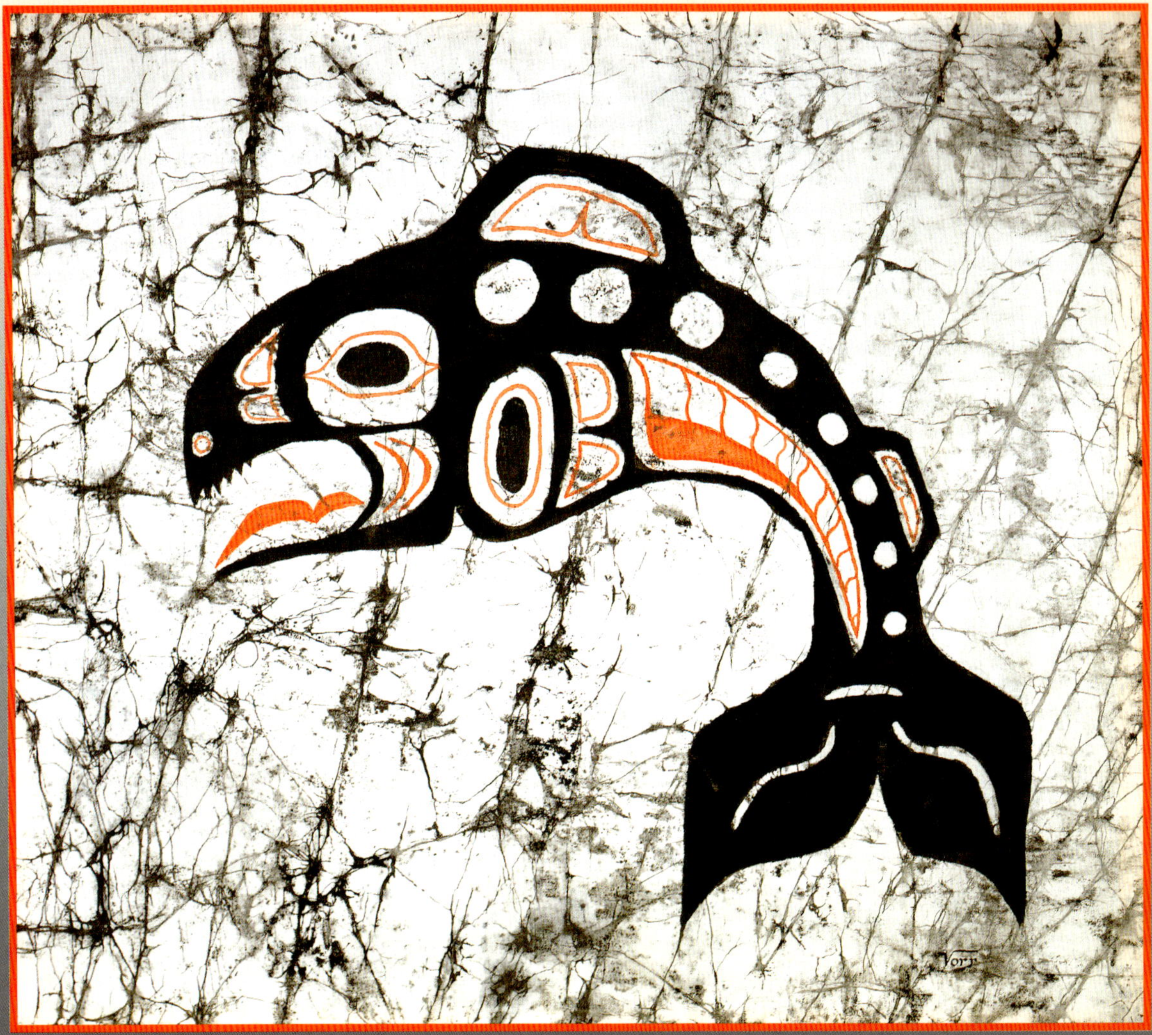
Vorr

Born of river and rock,
born of sea and sand;

salmon and whale
salmon and whale.

Killer Whale
by Veronica Orringram (Colville)
painted textile,
27" x 24", 1982

Plums soften in the bowl;
tomorrow they will be ready for wine.
Stories take shape in the mind;
I will write until nightfall.

When spring comes we write love-poems and haiku
on leaves, and
throw them into the river.
Our words dissolve to silence;
sugar in water.

The continent of her being
is surrounded by water;
our reflections float
in these bordering seas.

In the reminiscing of grasses
we become ourselves, and
with the voices of her lightning
we find completion
to our song.

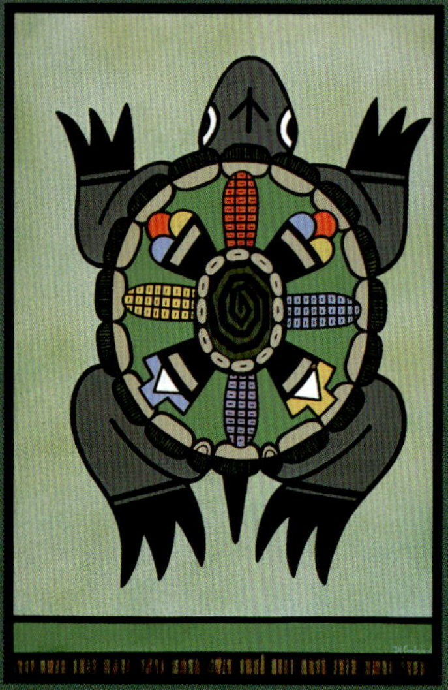

Turtle Design
by Delbert Coochsiwnkiomo (Hopi)
acrylic on canvas,
49″ x 37 ¹/₈″, 1975

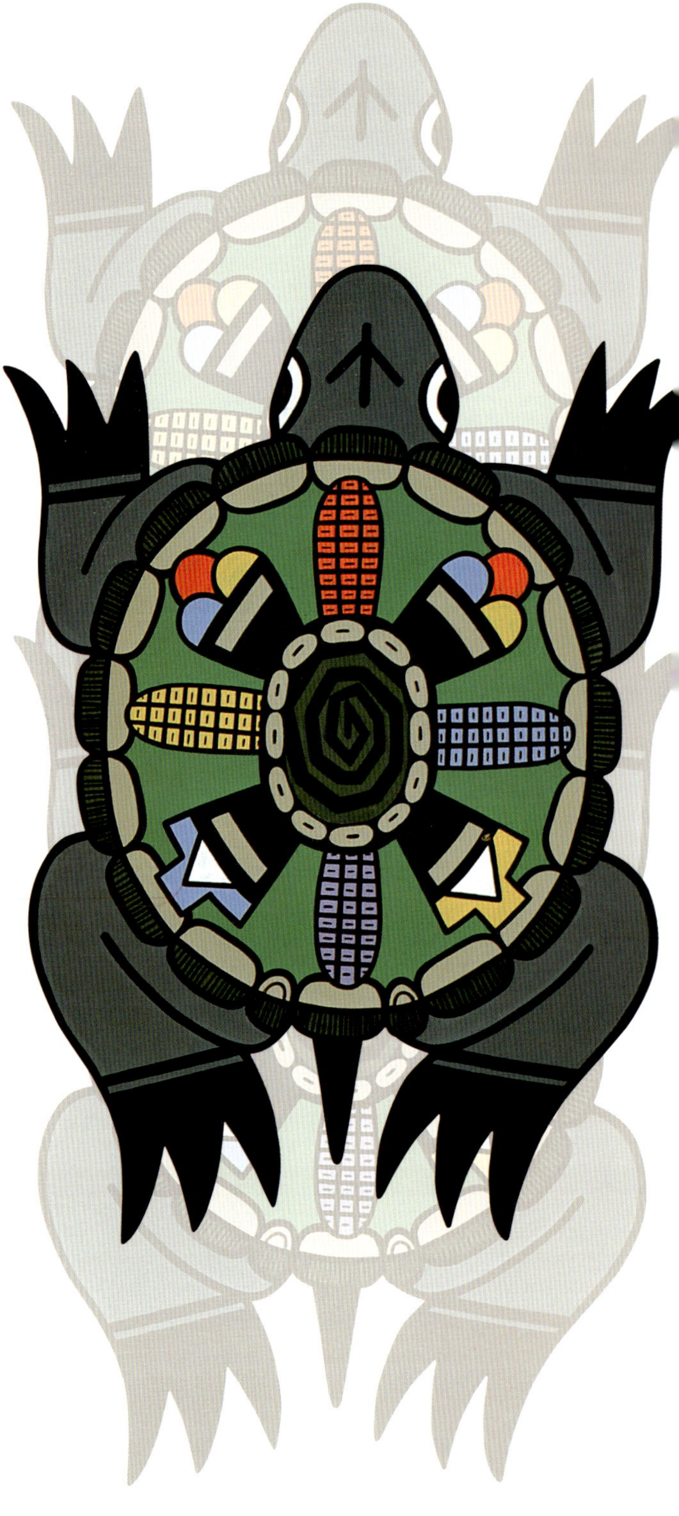

Clay pots dry
in warm autumn air.
Fresh ink waits;
there is a story coming.

*Small waves break on the shore;
each one a verse in nature's poem.*

*Shiny black pebbles
rest near our feet;
we also are part
of the poem.*

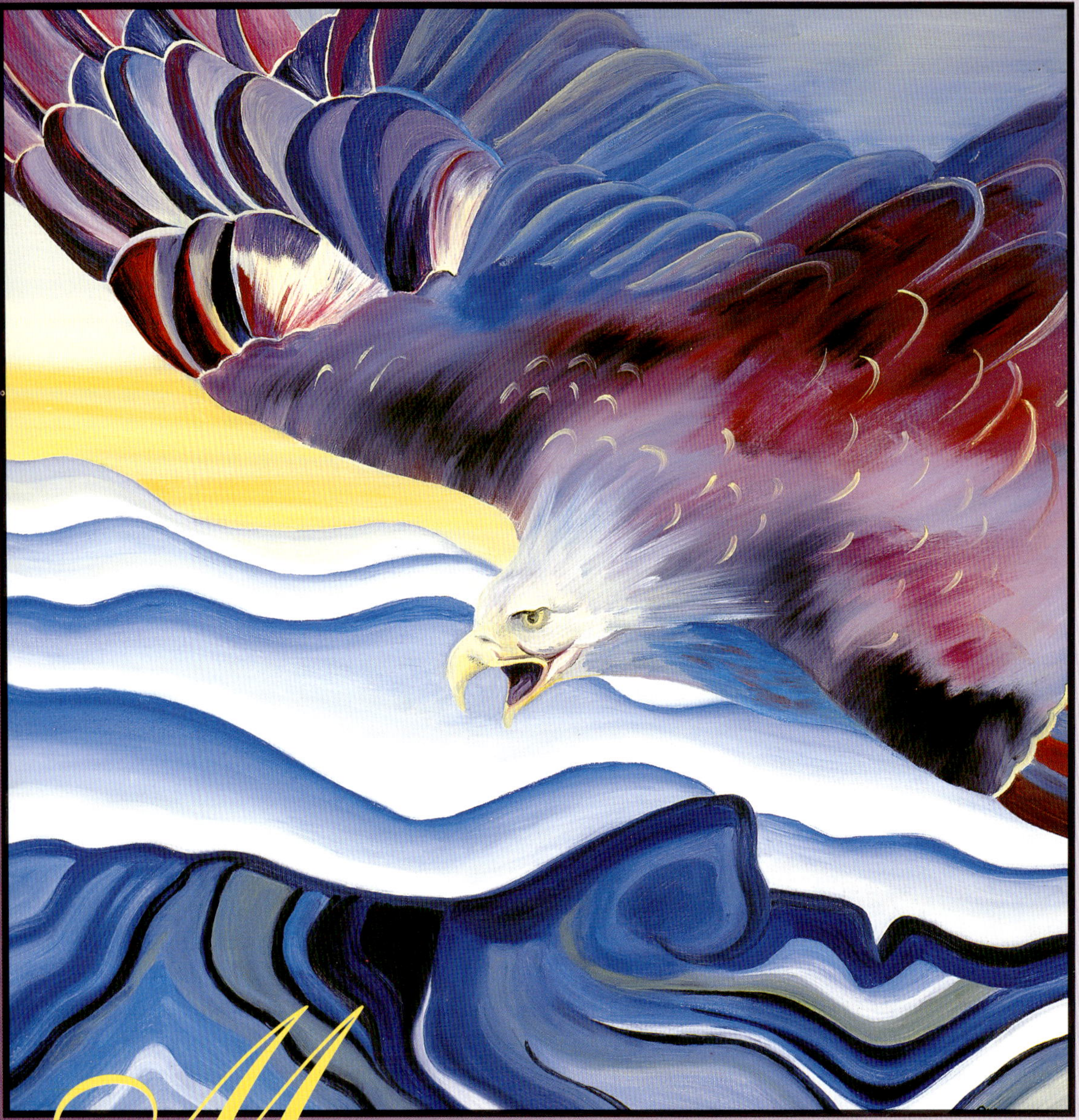

Memory drifts beyond
sky and cloud formations,
gliding through warm air,
spiraling very slowly downward
to become memory again

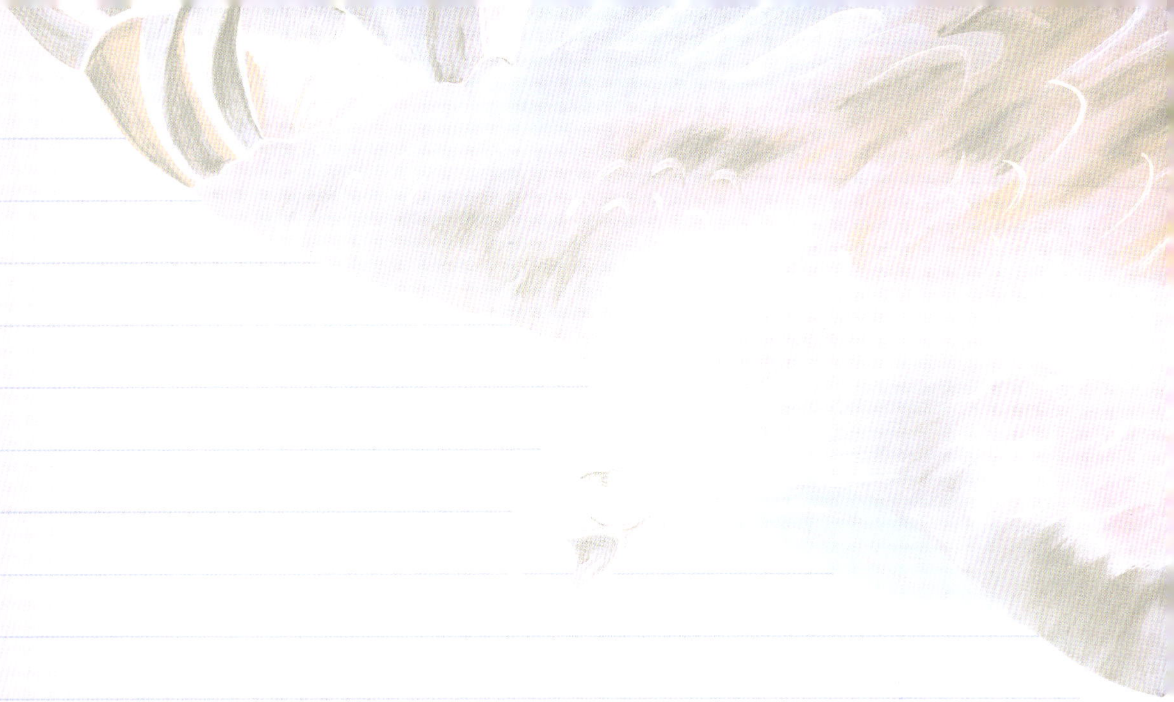

Eagle in Flight
by Cheryl Yellowhawk (Sioux)
oil on canvas,
21¾" x 21¾", 1985

*New moon rises;
there are a thousand poems to be written.
Midnight draws near;
one poem is complete.*

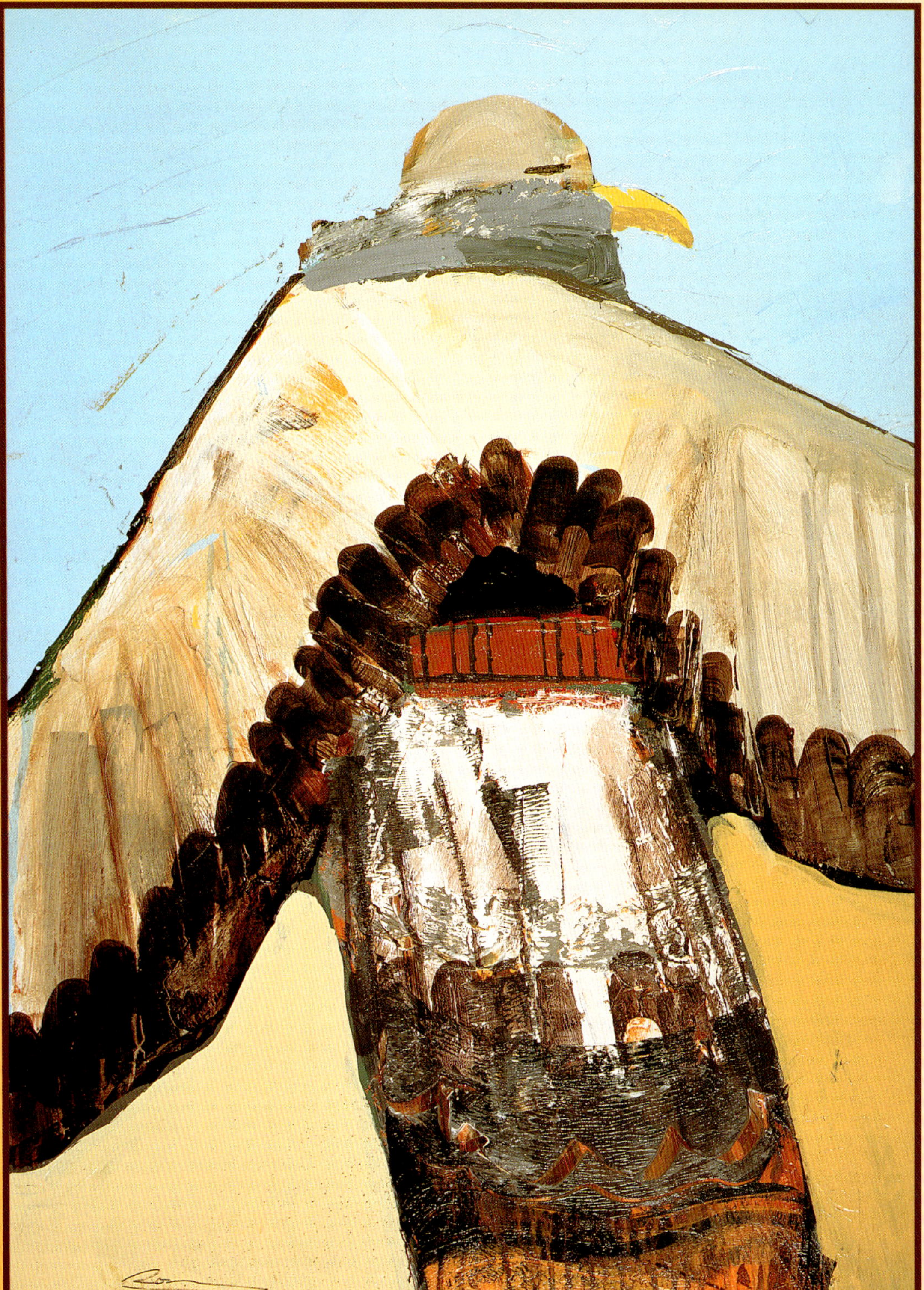

*E*agle dancer
transcends space and time.
Past, present and
future become one moment, connected through
each touch of moccasin to earth.

Eagle Dancer Between Heaven & Earth
by Mateo Romero (Cochiti)
acrylic on canvas,
38" x 28", 1991

Frost has settled
on the north-facing window's ledge.
Sun's first rays tell me
it is time
to set pen to paper.

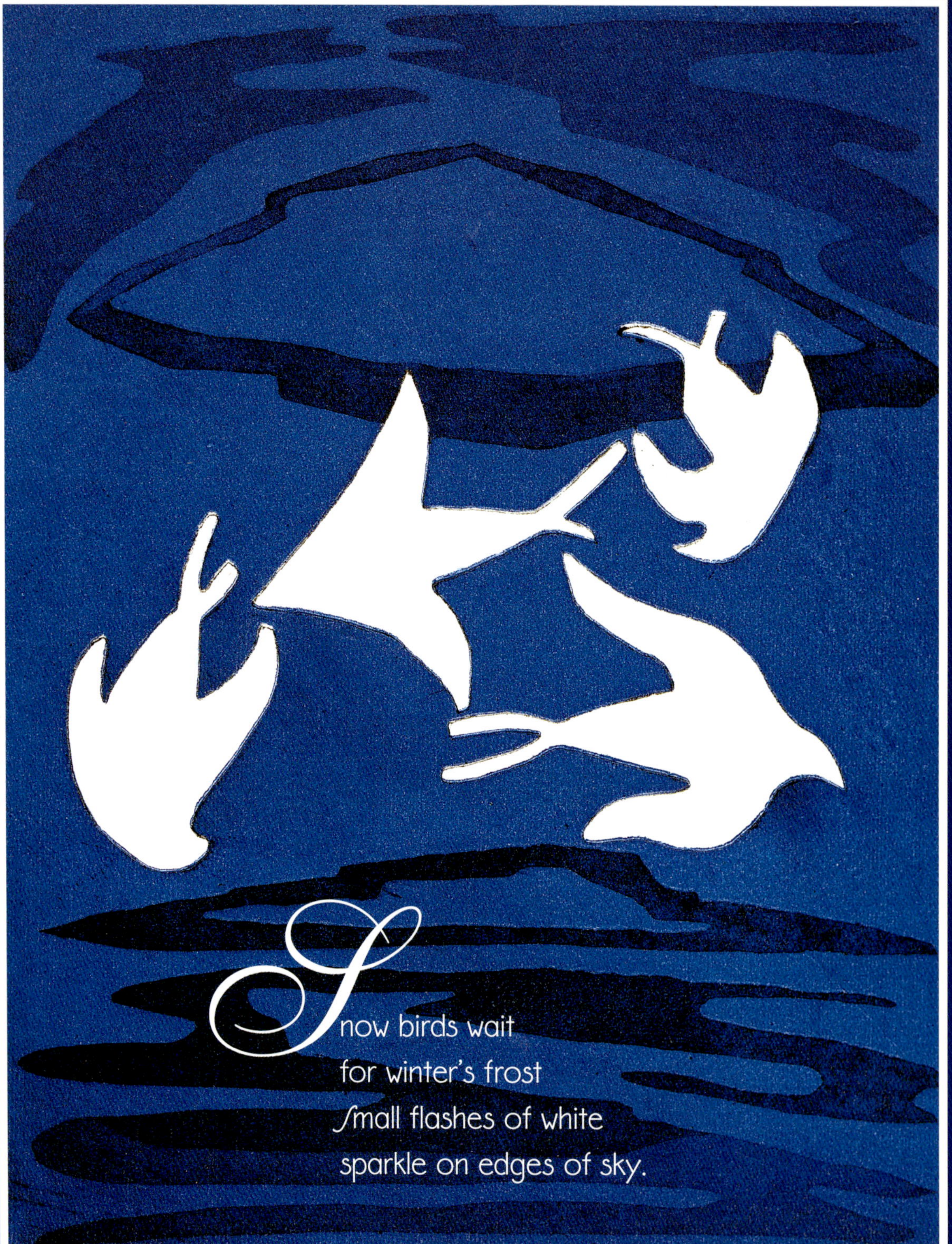

Snow birds wait
for winter's frost
Small flashes of white
sparkle on edges of sky.

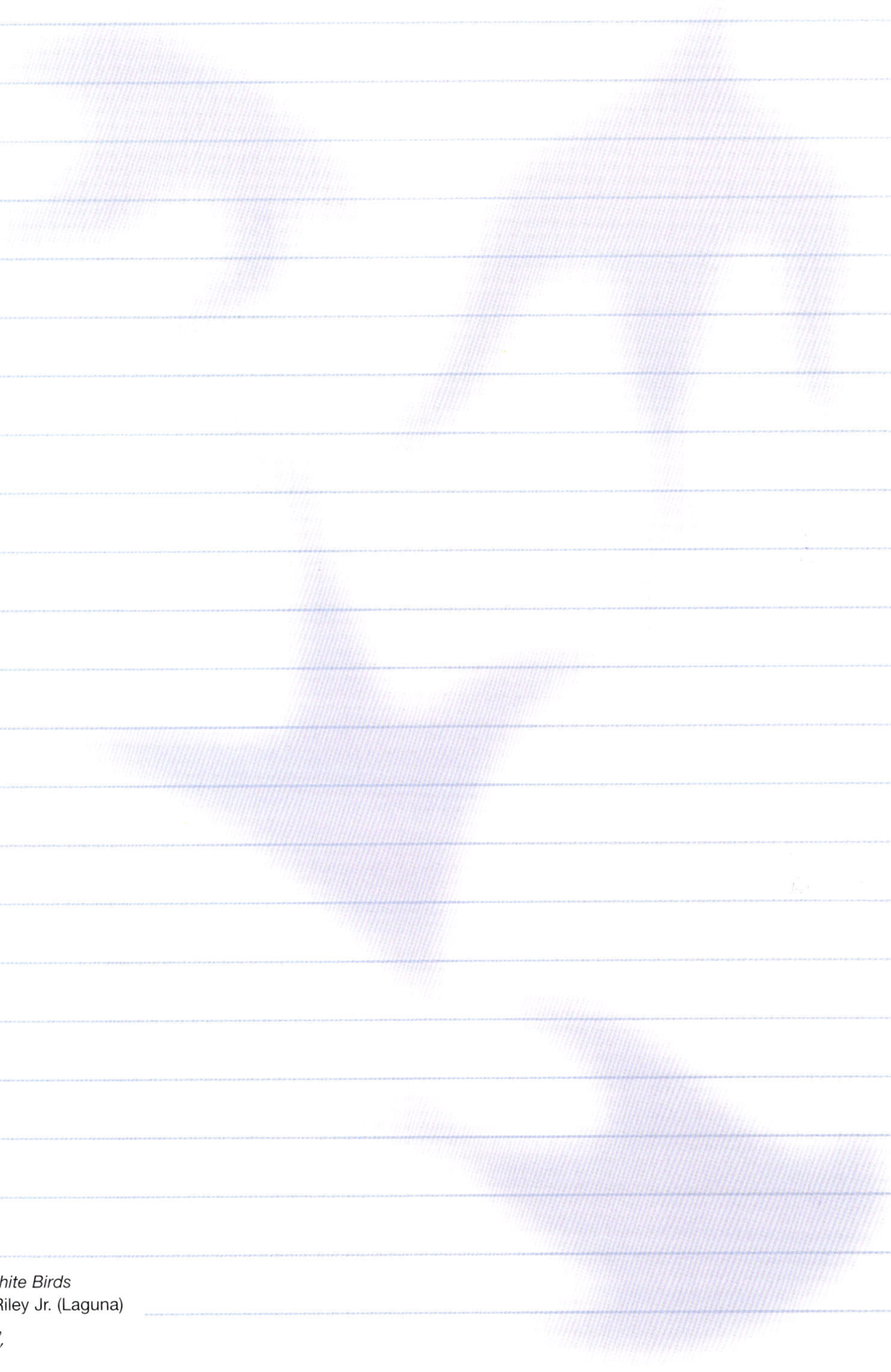

Blue with White Birds
by Joseph Riley Jr. (Laguna)
linocut print,
16 1/2″ x 13 1/4″

Tiny black ants follow one another across warm, white sand. No, wait...those are letters on the page!

IAIA

Institute of American Indian Arts

The Institute of American Indian Arts (IAIA) is pleased to share 19 of the nearly 6,500 objects of art in the National Collection of Contemporary Indian Art. The images in this writing journal are a modest indication of the talent and creativity of the 3,700 students from nearly all of the 558 federally recognized tribes who attended our college in the 20th century. These works represent the largest and most diverse collection of contemporary American Indian art in the world.

The publication of this journal is one facet of the IAIA initiative to provide American Indian and Alaska Native students with access to opportunities through higher education, time for students to study and immerse themselves in the unique cultural and artistic traditions of American Indian and Alaskan Native peoples. Sixty percent of the proceeds from the sale of this collection support student education and a long-term goal to expand our academic program.

Thank you for helping IAIA continue its "tradition of creativity."

For more information on the IAIA, or to pledge your support please contact:

The Institute of American Indian Arts

83 Avan Nu Po Road Santa Fe, NM 87505

1-800-804-6423   Web Site: www.iaiancad.org

Poetry: RoseMary Diaz
Tewa (Santa Clara Pueblo)
Design/Production:
Creative Works

Printed in Hong Kong
Publisher: Turtle Island
www.turtleisland.com
ISBN: 1-928816-09-6

TURTLE ISLAND
PUBLISHING

Following Page:
Textile
by Mike OneStar (Sioux)
Rayon,
46" x 174", 1976

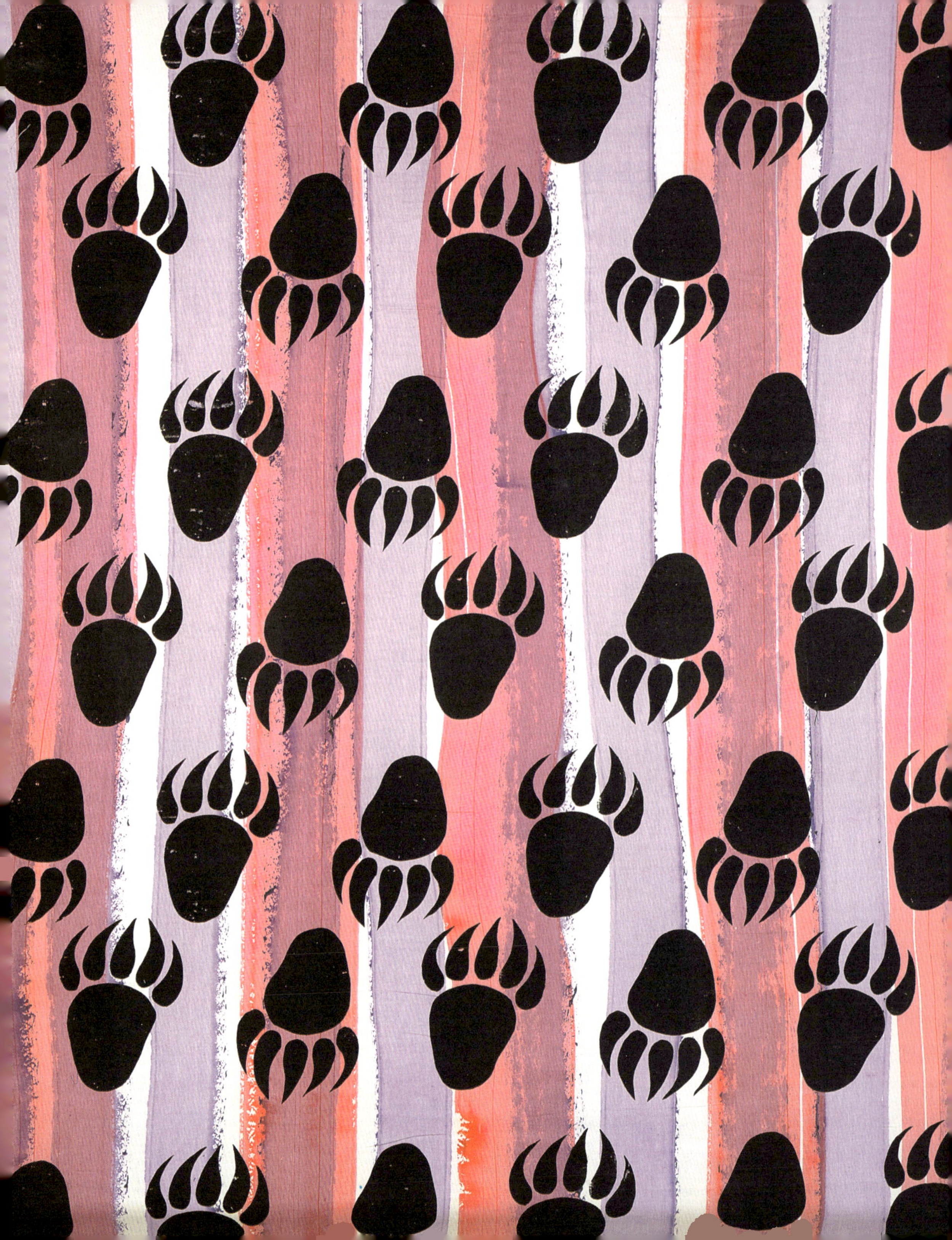